Knowledge Management

This shortform book presents key peer-reviewed research selected by expert series editors and contextualised by new analysis from each author on the subject of knowledge management in industrial history.

With contributions on knowledge management, knowledge transfer, knowledge loss, knowledge creation, competition and co-operation in producing skilled employees, and ownership structures and their relation to knowledge management, this volume provides an array of fascinating insights into industrial history.

Of interest to business and economic historians, this shortform book also provides analysis and illustrative case-studies that will be valuable reading across the social sciences.

John F. Wilson is Pro Vice-Chancellor (Business and Law) at Northumbria University at Newcastle. He has published widely in the fields of business, management and industrial history, including ten monographs, six edited collections and over seventy articles and chapters.

Ian Jones is Senior Research Assistant at Newcastle Business School, Northumbria University, and has previously won the John F. Mee Best Paper Award at the Academy of Management in 2018 for his contribution to the Management History Division.

Steven Toms is Professor of Accounting at the University of Leeds. He is former Editor of Business History. His research interests are focused on accounting and financial history and the history of the textile industry.

Routledge Focus on Industrial History

Series Editors: John F. Wilson, Steven Toms and Ian Jones

This shortform series presents key peer-reviewed research originally published in the *Journal of Industrial History*, selected by expert series editors and contextualised by new analysis from each author on how the specific field addressed has evolved.

Of interest to business historians, economic historians and social scientists interested in the development of key industries, the series makes theoretical and conceptual contributions to the field, as well as providing a plethora of empirical, illustrative and detailed case-studies of industrial developments in Britain, the United States and other international settings.

The Role of Governments in Markets
Interventions and Unexpected Consequences in Industrial History
Edited by John F. Wilson, Steven Toms and Ian Jones

A Search for Competitive Advantage
Case Studies in Industrial History
Edited by John F. Wilson, Steven Toms and Ian Jones

Knowledge Management
Dependency, Creation and Loss in Industrial History
Edited by John F. Wilson, Ian Jones and Steven Toms

The Development of Professional Management
Training, Consultancy, and Management Theory in Industrial History
Edited by John F. Wilson, Ian Jones and Steven Toms

For more information about this series, please visit: www.routledge.com/Routledge-Focus-on-Industrial-History/book-series/RFIH

Knowledge Management

Dependency, Creation and Loss in Industrial History

Edited by John F. Wilson, Ian Jones and Steven Toms

LONDON AND NEW YORK

First published 2022
by Routledge
2 Park Square, Milton Park, Abingdon, Oxon OX14 4RN

and by Routledge
605 Third Avenue, New York, NY 10158

Routledge is an imprint of the Taylor & Francis Group, an informa business

British Library Cataloguing-in-Publication Data
A catalogue record for this book is available from the British Library

Library of Congress Cataloging-in-Publication Data
Names: Wilson, John F., 1955– editor. | Jones, Ian (Senior research assistant), editor. | Toms, Steven, editor.
Title: Knowledge management : dependency, creation and loss in industrial history / edited by John F. Wilson, Ian Jones and Steven Toms.
Description: Abingdon, Oxon ; New York, NY : Routledge, 2022. | Series: Routledge focus on industrial history | Includes bibliographical references and index.
Identifiers: LCCN 2021013979 (print) | LCCN 2021013980 (ebook) | ISBN 9780367023911 (hardback) | ISBN 9781032077277 (paperback) | ISBN 9780429059001 (ebook)
Subjects: LCSH: Knowledge management—History. | Industrial management—History. | Industries—History.
Classification: LCC HD30.2 .K636874 2022 (print) | LCC HD30.2 (ebook) | DDC 658.4/038—dc23
LC record available at https://lccn.loc.gov/2021013979
LC ebook record available at https://lccn.loc.gov/2021013980

ISBN: 978-0-367-02391-1 (hbk)
ISBN: 978-1-032-07727-7 (pbk)
ISBN: 978-0-429-05900-1 (ebk)

DOI: 10.4324/9780429059001

Typeset in Times New Roman
by codeMantra

Contents

Figures

Tables

Maps

Contributors

Rolv Petter Amdam is Professor of Business History at BI Norwegian Business School. He has also been the Alfred D. Chandler Jr. International Scholar in Business History at Harvard Business School in 2015, a visiting fellow at the SCANCOR-Weatherhead Centre of International Affaïrs, Harvard, and a visiting fellow at the University of Reading. He has published extensively on business history, executive education, industrial clusters and globalization. He has written and edited several books on various topics, including the history of the glass industry, pharmaceutical companies, the aluminium industry and business schools.

Ove Bjarnar is Professor Emeritus of History at Molde University College – Specialized University in Logistics. He has published on regional economic history and industrial development, regional and cross-national managerial knowledge transfer, regional clusters and the societal role of women's organizations.

Robert Forrant is the University of Massachusetts Lowell Distinguished University Professor of History. His recent publications include *The Great Lawrence Textile Strike of 1912: New Scholarship on the Bread & Roses Strike* (2014); *The Big Move: Immigrant Voices from a Mill City*, with Christoph Strobel (2011); and *Metal Fatigue: American Bosch and the Demise of Metalworking in the Connecticut River Valley* (2009). He is working on two new books: *Lowell: The Worlds and Histories of a New England Mill City* (University of Massachusetts Press) and *Interpreting Labor and Working-Class History at Museums and Historic Sites*, with Mary Anne Trasciatti (University of Illinois Press).

Hallgeir Gammelsæter is Professor in the Department of Economics and Social Sciences at Molde University College – Specialized University in Logistics. He has published extensively on the sports organization and management, the football industry and innovation/knowledge management. He has published and edited several books including *Innovasjonspolitikkens scenografi (The Scenography of Innovation Politics)*, with Peter Arbo (2004); *The Organisation and Governance of Top Football Across Europe*, with Benoit Senaux (2011); and *Poeng, Penger og Politikk (Points, Pounds and Politics)* (2016).

Charles Harvey is Professor of Business History and Management and the Director of the Centre for Research on Entrepreneurship, Wealth, and Philanthropy at Newcastle University. He has published extensively on business history, historical organization studies, strategy, philanthropy and entrepreneurship. He has written and edited several books, including *Business Elites and Corporate Governance in France and the UK*, with Mairi Maclean (2006) and most recently *Historical Organization Studies: Theory and Applications* (2021), with Mairi Maclean, Stewart Clegg and Roy Suddaby.

Tony Hayward completed his PhD at Royal Holloway, University of London, with his thesis titled *The Growth and Development of the Japanese Electrical and Electronics Industry, 1945–94.*

Mairi Maclean is Professor of International Business at the University of Bath, UK. She received her PhD from the University of St Andrews. Her research interests include historical organization studies, business elites and elite power, and entrepreneurial philanthropy. Her research has been funded by the Leverhulme Trust, Reed Charity and the ESRC, and has been published in journals such as the *Academy of Management Review*, *Organization Studies* and *Human Relations*. Her most recent book is *Historical Organization Studies: Theory and Applications*, with Stewart Clegg, Roy Suddaby and Charles Harvey (London: Routledge).

Introduction

John Wilson, Ian Jones and Steven Toms

Purpose and significance of the series

The concept of the *Routledge Focus on Industrial History* series was motivated by the desire of the editors to provide an outlet for articles originally published in the defunct *Journal of Industrial History* (*JIH*). By using an extensive repository of top-quality publications, the series will ensure that the authors' findings contribute to recent debates in the field of management and industrial history. Indeed, the articles contained in these volumes will appeal to a wide audience, including business historians, economic historians and social scientists interested in longitudinal studies of the development of key industries and themes. Moreover, the series will provide fresh insight into how the academic field has developed over the past 20 years.

The editors believe that the quality of scholarship evident in the articles originally published in the *JIH* now deserve a much broader audience. The peer-reviewed articles are built on robust business-historical research methodologies and are subject to extensive primary research. The series will make important theoretical and conceptual contributions to the field and provide a plethora of empirical, illustrative and detailed case studies of industrial developments in the United Kingdom, the United States and other international settings. The collection will be of interest to a broad stratum of social scientists, especially business school and history department academics, because it provides valuable material that can be used in both teaching and research.

Building on the original *Journal of Industrial History*

The first edition of the *JIH* was published in 1998, with the aim of providing 'clear definitional parameters for industrial historians' and

DOI: 10.4324/9780429059001

in turn establishing links between 'industrial history and theoretical work in social science disciplines like economics, management (including international business), political science, sociology, and anthropology'. Because it has been more than 20 years since its original publication, it is clear that the relevance of the *JIH* has stood the test of time. The original *JIH* volumes covered a diverse range of topics, including industrial structure and behaviour, especially in manufacturing and services; industrial and business case studies; business strategy and structure; nationalization and privatization; globalization and competitive advantage; business culture and industrial development; education, training and human resources; industrial relations and its institutions; the relationship between financial institutions and industry; industrial politics, including the formulation and impact of industrial and commercial policy; and industry and technology. The current *Routledge Focus on Industrial History* series will provide a cross section of articles that cover a wide range themes and topics, many of which remain central to management studies. These include separate volumes: *Management and Industry*, *Banking and Finance* and *Growth and Decline of American Industry*. Future volumes in the series will cover case studies in the development of professional management, and the cotton and textile industry. The *Routledge Focus on Industrial History* series will reframe highly original material that illustrates a wide variety of themes in management and organization studies, including entrepreneurship, strategy, family business, trust, networks and international business, focusing on topics such as the growth of the firm, crisis management, governance, management and leadership.

Volume seven: contribution and key findings

The seventh volume of this series focuses on systems of knowledge management, including strategies for knowledge creation, knowledge retention and maintenance, and the effects of knowledge loss in industrial history. This volume examines a broad range of strategies related to managing knowledge and the effects of a successful, or unsuccessful, knowledge management system, ranging through the nineteenth and twentieth centuries spanning Japan, the United States, and Norway. The articles in this volume show the importance of knowledge management in various industries, how firms and nations have attempted to disseminate accrued knowledge to make the best use of it and the long-reaching effects of knowledge loss on firms and wider society.

The first chapter, 'From knowledge dependence to knowledge creation: Industrial growth and technological advance of the Japanese electronics industry' by Charles Harvey, Mairi Maclean and Tony Hayward, focuses on Japan's electronics industry development post-World War II. This chapter discusses attempts to differentiate between the proximate causes of Japan's economic recovery, such as domestic market factors and international economic factors, and the ultimate causes, such as the occupation of Japan and the systems of states-business relations that developed after World War II. This chapter then discusses how Japanese electronics firms moved from a position of knowledge dependence in the immediate aftermath of World War II to being knowledge creators by the 1990s. Business leaders were able to take advantage of unique economic, political and cultural forces by investing in their physical, human and technological resources in order to allow them to be successful in the market place which in turn enabled them to invest in the functions that would allow their firms to become knowledge creators.

The second chapter, 'Management qualifications and dissemination of knowledge in regional innovation systems: the case of Norway 1930s–1990s' by Ove Bjarnar, Rolv Petter Amdam and Hallgier Gammelsæter, discusses the Norwegian network of national, regional and local organizations that attempted to harness regional, international and academic knowledge, and disseminate it to businesses. These national, regional and local networks were made up of governmental departments, academic institutions and professional organizations, with the exact makeup and organization fluctuating over time. This network attempted to take the context-independent knowledge generated at academic institutions and transmit this to local businesses, where it could be combined with their local, context-dependent knowledge to improve the management quality and competitiveness of these firms. This chapter also shows the mixed levels of success of the network over time, with efforts to incorporate regional colleges into the network to provide local formal management education resulting in less knowledge dissemination to local businesses as the focus shifted towards formal education.

The final chapter, '"Neither a sleepy town nor a coarse factory town": Skill in the Greater Springfield Massachusetts industrial economy, 1800–1990' by Robert Forrant, focuses on the emergence of Springfield, Massachusetts, as a regional hub for engineering and manufacturing, and its decline in the twentieth century. This chapter shows how the decision to build the Springfield Armoury acted to draw skilled engineers to the local area, setting up their own manufactories to supply the military. These manufactories, and the Armoury itself, trained new engineers, ensuring a steady supply of skilled workers available who often had shared work experiences and were willing to cooperate across organizations to solve engineering problems. However, by the middle of the twentieth century, Springfield's industrial economy began to shrink, skill development became less prevalent, and technological innovation and sharing new production techniques between firms declined. This chapter also shows that the gradual change in ownership from local people to a more geographically distant group who did not value the skills and knowledge of the Springfield employees as an advantage over their competitors contributed to this decline. These new owners looked to lower production costs by moving production to areas with cheaper labour or through the replacement of skilled labour with machinery and automation.

Conclusion

It is apparent from this brief review of the chapters that the seventh volume in the series makes important contributions to the field of industrial history in several ways. Firstly, it provides a series of high-calibre and unique studies in aspects of industrial history that contribute to more recent debates on knowledge management within organizations, knowledge transfer, knowledge loss and knowledge creation. Secondly, the chapters shed light on the broader subjects of specialization, ownership and ownership structures, cooperation and competition, and the importance of education and experiential knowledge in the creation and operation of successful firms. Finally, this volume provides strong historical case studies that can be used by students and researchers who are exploring issues related to knowledge management in Norway, the United States and Japan; the effects on organizations of knowledge loss; and how firms can move from knowledge dependence to knowledge creation. The editors believe that this volume will not only provide a much wider audience for articles that link into a range of topical issues but also feed into debates in the wider social sciences. These are themes that will be developed further in subsequent volumes of the *Routledge Series of Industrial History*, highlighting the intrinsic value in republishing material from the *JIH* and ensuring that the articles contribute extensively to current debates.

From knowledge dependence to knowledge creation

Industrial growth and the technological advance of the Japanese electronics industry

Charles Harvey, Mairi Maclean and Tony Hayward

The rise of the Japanese economy from the rubble of defeat in the Second World War may no longer be viewed as 'miraculous', but it remains a phenomenon that is imperfectly understood.[1] Lewis, Fitzgerald and Harvey,[2] amongst others, have provided a convincing synthesis of the process of economic regeneration and development that resulted in an annual average compound rate of growth in real GDP between 1950 and 1992 of 6.7 per cent, a figure which dwarfs those for rival industrial economies such as Germany (4.3 per cent), France (3.8 per cent), the USA (3.3 per cent) and the UK (2.4 per cent).[3] On the supply side, Japan is seen to have benefited from a large, highly skilled and disciplined labour force that for long accepted relatively low wages in return for continuous employment. Equally, the Japanese demonstrated the importance of discipline and social restraint in preferring to save and invest rather than consume both at the individual and corporate levels.[4] Relatively low wages and the desire to save and accumulate combined to provide the wherewithal for capital investment and output growth on an unprecedented scale. On the demand side, Japanese industry was well positioned to take advantage of the postwar liberalization of the international economy and the western boom in consumption. Meanwhile, the domestic market, while not closed to foreigners, was informally protected to the extent that the producers of both consumer and industrial goods could more or less guarantee to recover development costs on the basis of domestic sales alone. Such favourable supply and demand conditions were necessary to rapid industrial growth, but they were not in themselves sufficient. What crucially made for success was that Japanese firms had what was needed to take advantage of favourable circumstances. They invested heavily in plant and equipment

DOI: 10.4324/9780429059001

to capture economies of scale and scope. They continuously refined methods of working to win productivity gains and improve product quality. They acquired and developed the technologies needed to introduce a stream of new products and manufacturing processes. And, finally, they created organizations with the flexibility to change and adapt to new circumstances and events, eventually moving beyond the shores of Japan to build international business empires.

This explanation of Japanese economic success in the postwar era, while conforming to the available macro- and micro-economic evidence, does not tell the whole story. As Maddison[5] has pointed out in a different context, it is important to distinguish between the *proximate* and *ultimate* causes of economic growth. Proximate causality refers to the inputs and techniques that directly bring about growth, whereas ultimate causality refers to the institutional, historical, cultural and policy factors that underlie the more immediate proximate causes. It is relatively easy to identify and quantify the impact of proximate causes of growth (the supply and demand side factors noted above, for example), but the ultimate causes of growth almost invariably remain more mysterious and less amenable to measurement. This is because when looking at the proximate we are mainly concerned with the hard and tangible outward expressions of a phenomenon, but when in search of ultimate causality, we are more concerned to discover historical determinants, institutional relationships and cultural origins, which are altogether more elusive, harder to circumscribe and pin down.

This article is concerned with one aspect of the search for a more complete understanding of the growth and development of the Japanese economy in the postwar period. The main topic is the creation of leading-edge technological capabilities within the Japanese electronics industry, one of the pillars of the postwar economy and an industrial success story of the first order. From a position of chronic depression at the end of the Second World War, the industry entered into a period of sustained development that proceeded virtually unbroken before the entry of the Japanese economy into stagnation during the early 1990s. Year-on-year growth, at rates in excess of 10 per cent for most years between 1950 and 1990, saw Japanese firms rise to the fore in international markets. In 1990, the value of output of the Japanese electronics industry was a staggering $164,854 million compared to $154,625 million for Europe as a whole and $211,471 million for North America. Within the field of consumer electronics, Japanese firms had won a massive advantage, with sales valued at $30,570 million compared to $12,271 million and $6,382 million for Europe and North America, respectively.[6]

In establishing themselves as global players, Japanese electronics firms moved over the years from a position of dependence on foreign technology to one of technological leadership. In this article, we explore how this transformation was achieved and how Japanese electronics firms have learned to control and exploit knowledge creating systems and processes. We distinguish throughout between the proximate and ultimate sources of industrial growth. In particular, we seek to establish the multi-faceted context and complex set of relationships that have conditioned strategic decision making and the creation of technological capabilities. We begin by analyzing the proximate causes of industrial growth and put forward a simple interpretive model. In Section 3, the analysis is deepened through a discussion of the ultimate (historical, cultural and political) sources of industrial growth. This enables us in Section 4 to contextualize and explain the movement from knowledge dependence to knowledge creation. We conclude in Section 5 by analyzing the outcomes and implications of the growth and technological advance of the Japanese electronics industry since 1945.

1 Proximate Causes of Growth and Development

In our view, the postwar growth and development of the Japanese electronics industry is best represented as the product of dynamic evolutionary forces, complexity and multicausality matched by the existence over the years of a relatively small number of industry constants. On the one hand, complexity may be seen to have resulted from the interplay of macro and micro forces and domestic and international developments. On the other hand, the powerful upward trajectory of the industry over more than four decades, to become established at the forefront of the global industry, may be represented as the product of four mutually reinforcing forces, each of which has varied in intensity and importance from time to time. The four determinants of corporate and industrial performance and the manner of their interaction are presented in Figure 1.

The model, while abstracting from reality, has the virtue of demonstrating that electronics enterprises and management teams existed in a particular historical context, which *ipso facto* conditioned strategic choices. It has the further advantage of providing a scheme for the classification of the main factors governing the long-term performance of the industry. In all, twelve main factors may be identified as key proximate causes of growth and development.

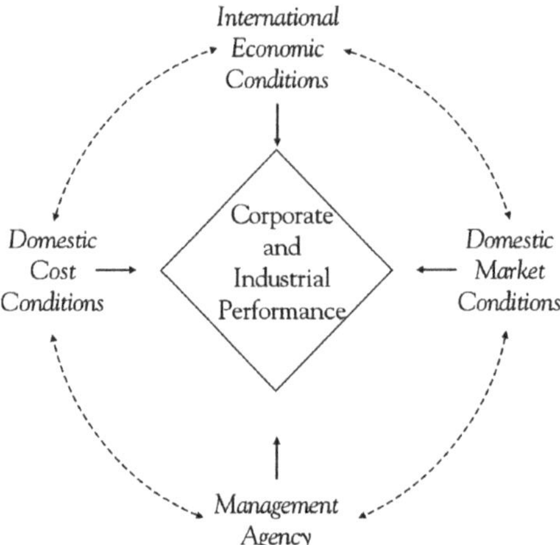

Figure 1.1 The Japanese electronics industry: determinants of corporate and industrial performance

Domestic Cost Factors

Japanese firms had the advantage down to the 1970s of relatively low wages and a low labour share of value added.[7] This conferred the twin advantages of being able to manipulate prices competitively while yielding substantial retained earnings to fund large-scale investments.

From the early 1950s onwards, Japanese firms benefited from having a highly disciplined and committed workforce, reluctant to jeopardize firms' wellbeing through strike action or to restrict output and productivity growth.[8] The existence of a dedicated and responsive labour force allowed firms to take full advantage of innovations in methods and systems of production without conceding all the gains to labour in the form of higher wages and improved conditions of employment.

High rates of corporate and individual savings created a situation of abundant capital at low cost, which in turn facilitated the pursuit of economies of scale and scope through massive investments in production, research and development (R&D), and marketing.[9]

Domestic Market Factors

The domestic market for electronic goods benefited from a high-income elasticity of demand for its products when for several decades the rate of growth of Japan's GNP considerably exceeded that of its main rivals.[10]

While the domestic markets for consumer and industrial electronics were buoyant, they were in part protected from foreign competition by the continuation of Japanese import restrictions. This meant that domestic prices could be kept high and that domestic sales alone could underwrite heavy investments in new product development, plant and equipment.[11]

International Economic Factors

The postwar international political settlement favoured Japan by giving ready access to overseas markets despite a lack of reciprocity. Hence, the toleration displayed by western countries down to the 1980s of high and rising Japanese manufacturing trade surpluses.[12]

The significant undervaluation of the yen against the dollar during the era of fixed exchange rates gave Japanese electronics a big competitive advantage in overseas markets, stimulating the pursuit of high export ratios and scale economies.[13]

Japan, before it was seen to be a major rival, was granted ready access to crucial western technologies (as well as management expertise) through licensing and other agreements. Without access to leading-edge technologies during the critical formative period of the modern electronics industry in the 1950s and 1960s, the Japanese electronics industry could not have embarked on the expansionist international path that it took.[14]

Internal Firm Factors

Industry leaders pursued a logic-of-action similar to that identified by Chandler in *Scale and Scope*,[15] recognizing at an early stage the need to make massive investments in production, distribution and management in order to compete successfully in international markets. The internalization of this view by management led firms continuously to upgrade their knowledge base, systems, processes, human resources, capital stock and product range.

Control of key product and production technologies was seen at an early stage to be crucial to long-term success within the global electronics industry. Initially through licensing, but fairly soon thereafter through self-generated R&D, Japanese firms reaped the rewards of technological excellence.[16]

High-quality standards and responsiveness to customer needs were established as core industrial values during the postwar reconstruction period. The belief that the customer always has new needs, and that it is necessary for firms proactively to identify and satisfy these, has led to numerous product innovations and the securing of economies of scope in production and distribution.[17]

Japanese managers within the electronics industry have responded with alacrity to fundamental shifts in competitive conditions. The massive transfer of production of consumer electronics from domestic to offshore locations is but one of numerous examples of a deep-seated understanding that individual firms must work with and not against the logic of the market.[18]

The critical point to emerge from this taxonomy of the proximate sources of growth and development is that individual firms and business leaders were neither passive beneficiaries of uniquely favourable circumstances nor were they alone responsible for the success enjoyed by the Japanese electronics industry. What they must be credited with is discerning at critical moments what was required to take full advantage of new technologies and market opportunities and to act accordingly in making a long series of bold strategic investments. In practice, of course, it is not possible to isolate the impact of one factor or determinant from another, as the dashed lines in Figure 1 indicate. The situation is more akin to that described by Porter in *The Competitive Advantage of Nations*,[19] wherein mutually reinforcing interactions generate the momentum to create globally competitive industry clusters.

2 Ultimate Causes of Growth and Development

Any search for the ultimate causes of corporate and industrial growth involves studying the motivation and behaviour of economic actors at the level of both the individual and the organization. Inevitably these are mediated at the societal level through more general economic, cultural and political processes. All events and outcomes are in this sense historically contingent. From this viewpoint, a business enterprise is conceived primarily as a community dedicated to the maintenance and development of a value-creating system. The community is shaped and conditioned by environmental pressures and by the values and aspirations of its members, who in turn are influenced through their involvement with others in society. Corporate culture is defined as the shared values, beliefs and aspirations of members of the community, which find expression in the way they routinely behave and cooperate (or not) with others by way of formal and informal relationships.[20] The answers to ultimate questions, such as how and why business enterprises at a particular point in history form an enduring social settlement (the division of value added between capital and labour), can only be found through the analysis of historical, political and cultural processes.

It is difficult now, more than half a century later, to comprehend the depth of despair felt in Japan at the dramatic conclusion of the Second World War. Hyperinflation, mass unemployment and occupation followed, and it was not until the early 1950s that the country could look forward once again to a brighter future.[21] The details of how the Japanese people came to terms with defeat and rebuilt their nation and its place in the international community are beyond the scope of this article. However, the argument presented here is fundamentally informed by our understanding of some of the most salient stylized facts of postwar Japanese history.

Occupation and Economic Reconstruction

In pursuing its twin political objectives of demilitarization and the establishment of democracy, the Occupation administration actively promoted the economic reconstruction of Japan between 1945 and 1952. Most conspicuously, steps were taken to reform the old *zaibatsu* and the managerial class was purged of industrial leaders stained by association with militarism.[22] More importantly, it is accepted that economic expansion was needed to legitimize the new democratic pro-American political order. The electronics industry was a natural candidate for assistance through the agency of its Civil Communications Section, which promoted schemes for technical assistance and the introduction of modern management techniques under the banner of the quality movement. These initiatives had long lasting effects, anticipating the high profile work of management gurus like Deming, Juran and Drucker, and were consolidated between 1955 and 1962 through the work of the US technical assistance programme. Influential agencies such as the Electronics Industry Association of Japan (1948) and the Japan Productivity Center (1954) had their origins in American quality, productivity and technology initiatives.[23]

Japan and the International Economic Order

Japan suffered from a chronic balance of payments deficit for more than a decade after the end of the Second World War, notwithstanding the boost to exports resulting from the special procurements (*tokuju*) boom induced by the outbreak of the Korean War in June 1950. This was perceived in Washington as a fundamental threat to political and economic stability in Japan at a time when fear of communism was far from subsiding.[24] It is for this reason that the United States gave its blessing to the Foreign Exchange and Trade Control Law of 1949 and the Foreign Investments Law of 1950 that together provided a considerable degree of protection to nascent Japanese industries. Informal but effective protectionism was tolerated long after Japan had joined the IMF (International Monetary Fund) (1952) and had formally acceded to GATT (General Agreement on Tariffs and Trade) (1955). Even when the Japanese balance of payments swung into massive surplus, the infant industries having grown up, the US government continued to look benignly on the situation: the political gains from stability in Japan were seen to outweigh the economic costs.[25] Against the prevailing economic logic, the yen remained pegged at 360 to the dollar down to 1971, yielding a massive cost advantage to Japanese exporters.[26] Only after the Plaza Accord of 1985 was the situation fully normalized.[27]

Reconciliation of Capital and Labour

The history of labour relations in Japan in the first decade after the war is one of searing conflict followed by healing compromise. Labour was very much in the ascendancy during the crisis-torn hyperinflationary years (1945–49) when Japan's political future hung in the balance. Management sought to reclaim lost ground over the next few years, asserting its right to manage, and dismissing large numbers of workers following a series of calamitous strikes. The damage wrought by management-union antagonism served as a potent reminder of the costs of conflict, and as the economy stabilized in the early 1950s, both employers associations and unions began to see virtue in a more conciliatory approach to wage bargaining.[28] The 'new deal' settlement, seen nowadays as a quintessential part of the Japanese system, was established during the 1950s as a consensus emerged that capital and labour should work together in pursuit of prosperity. Relative stability of employment was guaranteed in exchange for corporate loyalty and recognition of the efficacy of mutual consultation. By the mid-1950s, the old politicized unions had given way to newer enterprise unions that stressed the unity of purpose binding the firm. There were two main consequences. First, the share of value added (sales minus purchases) distributed to labour in wages and salaries was much lower in Japan than in competitor nations. Correspondingly, a relatively high proportion of earnings was available for investment. Second, the 'new deal' social settlement prioritized long-term growth over short-term profit maximization in order to keep the workforce in continuous employment.[29]

Corporate Governance and Business-State Relations

Before the Second World War, a lack of adequate market mechanisms caused firms in many sectors to internalize activities within conglomerate structures. At the heart of several *zaibatsu* was a large bank, while associated general trading companies, the *sogoshosha*, provided access to raw material and overseas markets. The *zaibatsu* were formally disbanded after 1945 as part of the demilitarization process, but the economic logic of cooperative alliances encouraged the same groups to re-coalesce as *kigyo shudan* (enterprise groups). Mutual shareholdings created a fresh network of supportive strategic alliances, and company groups continued to facilitate investment and the flow of market intelligence in the reconstruction period and beyond.[30] The ability of large corporations, the *kaisha*, to attract the support of banks, business allies and government facilitated rapid industrialization in postwar Japan.[31] Government, through the agency of the Ministry of International Trade and Industry (MITI) and other bodies, was able to exert strategic influence through a process of administrative guidance (*gyosei shido*), striking a balance between cooperation and competition.[32] The system served to highlight and define strategic issues and to target resources in a flexible and effective manner.[33] This was a classic response to the problem of relative economic backwardness and the struggle to catch up with more advanced competitor nations. As the economy developed and companies upgraded their organizational capabilities, they became progressively less in need of support from the banks and state agencies.[34]

Economies of Scale and Scope

In *Scale and Scope*,[35] the classic study of the dynamics of industrial capitalism, Chandler makes the case that enterprises grow large and prosper when they remain focused and committed to the exploitation of economies of scale and scope. According to this view, large-scale investments are often needed in order to capture fully economies of scale in production, distribution and marketing, and to recoup R&D costs. Firms that exploit opportunities to win a significant market share through driving down unit prices while maintaining product quality secure sustainable first-mover advantages. These arise through reputation effects and because profits flow thick and fast for those that move first to capture scale economies. High profits mean that first-movers can reinvest heavily to keep ahead of the competition and diversify harmoniously to capture economies of scope (spreading R&D costs yet more thinly). Such firms enter a virtuous circle in which each sizeable new investment in physical, human and intellectual resources builds organizational capabilities and in turn the cash needed to sustain corporate growth and development. In confirming the applicability of the Chandler model to postwar Japan, Morikawa has demonstrated how the managerial elite that rose to prominence after 1945 pursued this logic-of-action and gave immediate priority to capital investment and building organizational capabilities rather than short-term profit maximization. Investments in plant, equipment and distribution were made on an unprecedented scale. A virtuous circle ensued: 'increasing equipment investment led to market expansion, which generated new business opportunities, stimulated competition for market share, and encouraged further equipment expansion'.[36]

These stylized facts embrace many of the ultimate causes of Japanese economic growth in the postwar period. Our list is not exhaustive nor is our account complete. But what we can say with confidence is that industrial success on the scale achieved was the product of a unique combination of historical circumstances. The Occupation administration strove for economic regeneration as a means of achieving political goals, and by the same token Japan was granted an advantageous position in the international economic order. High rates of corporate and personal savings, promoted by a social settlement between capital and labour that favoured accumulation over consumption, provided the means by which industrialists could take advantage of favourable domestic and international market conditions. The prevailing system of corporate governance, reinforced by supportive government agencies, encouraged a coordinated and strategically astute approach to corporate and industrial growth. Japan's new managerial class had a strong predilection for growth, investing heavily to secure economies of scale and scope, to win commanding market shares, and ultimately to build formidable organizational capabilities.[37]

Each of these forces was at play in creating the technologically sophisticated Japanese electronics industry of today. Companies such as Hitachi, Mitsubishi Electrical, NCR Japan, NEC, Nippon Columbia, Pioneer, Sharp, SMK, Stanley Electric, Tamura, TDK, Matsushita and Toshiba survived the tribulations of the Second World War, but the transition from war to peace was initially a slow and demanding process. However, some bright spots did emerge at an early stage encouraged by government and the Occupation administration. By the late 1940s, for example, there were some 200 companies contesting radio receiver production. Indeed, radio manufacturing had almost regained its 1941 wartime peak by 1948, and production levels escalated from 287,000 sets in 1950 to 10.2 million sets in 1959. The record of monochrome TV production tells a similar story of year-on-year growth with the number of sets produced rising from just 14,384 in 1953 to 2,872,209 in 1959. From virtually a standing start in 1945–46, the industry was producing goods to the value of Y391.5m by 1960 and already 16 per cent of sales were made abroad.[38]

It was after 1960, however, that the Japanese industry mounted a serious challenge to its American and European rivals in international markets. Output and exports forged ahead once firms had achieved mastery of solid-state technologies.[39] The figures presented in Tables 1 and 2 paint a remarkable picture. These suggest that the years between 1960 and 1995 may be divided into three periods. First, the period of super-fast growth between 1960 and the slowdown induced by the oil crisis of 1973. It is conspicuous that for electronics manufacturers at least, the oil crisis bit harder in domestic markets than it did internationally. Continued strong export growth buoyed up the industry such that growth rates remained positive even during the darkest of times. Thus during the second period, from 1973 to 1985, high rates of growth in output were underpinned by the industry's strong performance in export markets. There is an evident change in pattern during the third period, the decade following the Plaza Accord of 1985 that was marked by the phenomenon of yen appreciation. As the yen climbed steeply in value against the US dollar, Japanese electronic products became steadily less competitive in export markets and there

Table 1.1 Output and exports of the domestic Japanese electronics industry, 1960–95 (1990=100)

Year	*Output*		*Exports*	
	Current Prices	*1990 Prices*	*Current Prices*	*1990 Prices*
1960	1.6	1.2	0.6	0.4
1965	2.7	2.2	1.9	1.6
1970	12.2	10.3	7.2	6.1
1975	18.1	13.0	15.5	11.2
1980	36.1	26.3	38.5	28.1
1985	77.5	60.3	88.2	68.6
1990	100.0	100.0	100.0	100.0
1995	94.1	116.0	105.5	130.1

Sources: Computed from annual volumes of Bureau of Statistics, *Japan Statistical Yearbook*; and annual volumes of Ministry of International Trade and Industry, *Foreign Trade of Japan*.

Table 1.2 Average annual percentage rates of growth of Japanese electronics domestic output and exports, 1960–95

Year	*Output*		*Exports*	
	Current Prices	*1990 Prices*	*Current Prices*	*1990 Prices*
1960–65	10.6	15.5	26.2	29.3
1965–70	35.2	35.6	31.1	31.4
1970–75	8.3	4.8	16.6	12.8
1975–80	14.8	15.1	20.0	20.3
1980–85	16.5	18.1	18.0	19.6
1985–90	5.2	10.6	2.5	7.8
1990–95	–1.2	3.0	1.1	5.4

Sources: Computed from annual volumes of Bureau of Statistics, *Japan Statistical Yearbook*; and annual volumes of Ministry of International Trade and Industry, *Foreign Trade of Japan*.

was a commensurate downward pressure on profit margins. Manufacturers responded by shipping production offshore to the low-wage developing economies of South East Asia and mainland China. Hence, the sharp downturn in growth rates for output and exports, especially after 1990 when economic stagnation at home marked the end of the golden era of the Japanese electronics industry.

3 From Knowledge Dependence to Knowledge Creation

The powerful upward movement in production and exports recorded by the Japanese electronics industry over successive decades may give the impression of a simple yet compelling logic at work. But nothing could be further from the truth. Sustained growth over a long period was, in this instance, more the manifestation of effective structural change and adaptability than the persistent exploitation on a global scale of a limited number of markets. In fact, the industry displayed a remarkable capacity to re-invent itself in the face of cost and market imperatives. There have been profound changes in the balance of production within the domestic industry. In 1960, the industry was primarily identified with the production of consumer goods such as radios and televisions; by 1995, the situation was almost completely transformed. The long-term thrust recorded in Table 3 has been to foster the production of high value-added industrial equipment and electronic components. Meanwhile, the assembly of consumer products

Table 1.3 Sectoral shares of domestic output and exports of the Japanese electronics industry, 1960–95 (percentages)

Year	*Output*			*Exports*		
	Consumer	*Industrial*	*Components*	*Consumer*	*Industrial*	*Components*
1960	57	11	32	na	na	na
1965	51	22	27	na	na	na
1970	49	28	23	na	na	na
1975	36	38	26	51	25	24
1980	34	35	31	48	20	32
1985	26	41	33	39	30	31
1990	18	47	35	24	31	45
1995	11	47	42	11	26	63

Sources: Computed from annual volumes of Bureau of Statistics, *Japan Statistical Yearbook*; and annual volumes of Electronics Industries Association of Japan, *Facts and Figures*.

has been moved to lower wage economies offshore, especially after 1985.[40] Hence, the sudden surge in components as a proportion of exports after that date.

Fundamental to the process of long-term structural change within the industry was the increasing mastery of Japanese firms of relevant technologies and scientific knowledge, without which it would have been impossible to progress from a position of knowledge dependency to one of knowledge creation. The ability to acquire, control, utilize and commodify technological knowledge became assimilated over time as one of the core competencies of individual firms and the industry as a whole. This development has been depicted elsewhere as a series of distinct stages. Westney,[41] for example, identifies the 1950s and 1960s with technology imports, the 1970s with improvements in production technologies and quality, and the 1980s with domestically generated technologies and basic research. In our view, any such view is fundamentally flawed and misleading: both the nature of the process at work and the available empirical evidence defy such ready classification. At the level of the industry as a whole, the transformation process was progressive and more akin to continuous improvement than a series of staged paradigm shifts.

This view is implicit in the ‘mountain climbing’ metaphor of the technological advance of the Japanese electronics industry put forward by Makoto Kikuchi,[42] one-time Managing Director of Sony’s corporate research centre. A modified and updated Kikuchi ‘model’ is presented in Figure 2.

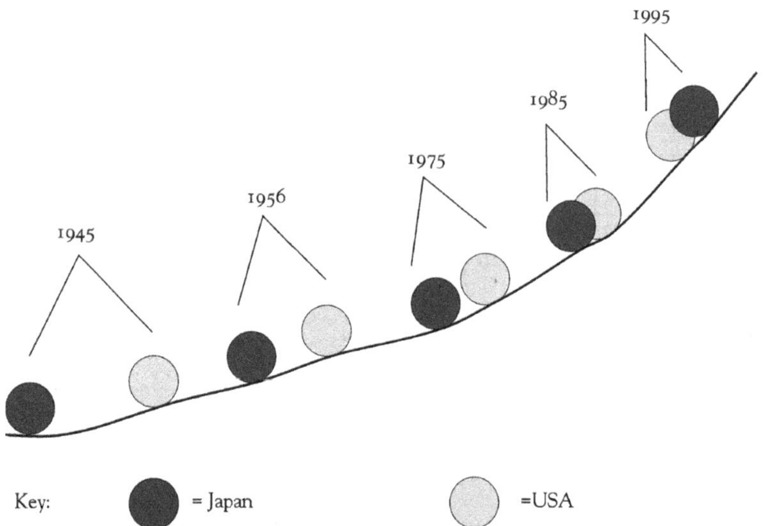

Figure 1.2 The 'mountain climbing' metaphor of technological progress within the non-military Japanese electronics industry

Source: Adapted from an original idea by Makota Kikuchi (one-time Managing Director of the Sony Research Centre).

The 'model', though highly subjective, is useful in drawing attention to a number of important points. First, the US electronics industry throughout the postwar period served as the technological exemplar for Japan: it is in the United States that standards traditionally have been set and key technologies developed, refined and commercialized, establishing the benchmarks against which Japanese firms have measured their success in closing the 'technology gap'.[43] Second, both the US and the Japanese industries have lived through a protracted period of technological development, distinguished by intensive organizational learning and the creation of fresh technological capabilities ('climbing the mountain').[44] Third, for a long period, down to the mid-1980s and the triumph of very large scale integration (VLSI), the Japanese industry was on balance playing 'catch-up' with the American industry. Fourth, the process of technological change, involving as it has done very large numbers of products and processes, in aggregate has been incremental rather than involving sudden shifts or movements. The pattern is one of progressively rising technological complexity, interdependence and sophistication.[45] Fifth, Japanese firms have moved forward from a low base more rapidly than their US rivals, taking the lead in many fields (liquid crystal displays, flash memories and professional broadcasting equipment, for example), to achieve an overall position of technological leadership within the non-military world industry.

The ultimate causes of the technological advance of the postwar Japanese electronics industry, moving from knowledge dependence to knowledge creation, are intimately bound up with the business history of modern Japan. Modern economic growth began following the Meiji restoration in 1868 and the exposure of the country to foreign ideas and influences. Mechanisms were developed, in part unique to Japan, which compensated for the lack of efficient markets and widespread manufacturing know-how. The state and its allies in business drove forward a modernizing agenda that in the 1930s became distorted by militarization and imperial ambitions. Notwithstanding, managerial and technological skills were accumulated and these were deployed to the full in the service of the military during the Second World War.[46] Japan's economic heroes, like their military colleagues, were humbled by defeat. Between 1945 and 1947, the Occupation administration actively remodeled business enterprises, government and university departments along civilian lines, terminating all activities that might serve military ends.[47] Numerous engineers and scientists joined the ranks of the unemployed.

Yet, whatever the immediate problems of adjusting from war to peace, Japan, like Germany, emerged from the war with a worthy industrial legacy in the form of established 'high technology' companies, business managers and engineering talent.[48] The main economic problems faced by Japan in 1945 were macroeconomic, political and structural, not corporate *per se*, although there were serious adverse consequences for business resulting from inflation, low levels of effective demand and a strident labour movement. Once these problems were resolved, however, Japanese electronics firms were well placed to confront the problem of relative technological backwardness that had existed before the war but which had been exacerbated by it. Furthermore, after 1947 and the issue of the Truman doctrine, the US government turned from foe to friend in actively promoting the transfer of technology and manufacturing know-how from the United States to Japan.[49] Military applications of American technology may have been banned, but this only served to concentrate resources and speed the rate of effective technology transfer.

Technology transfer was one element of a national strategy for the industrial recovery of Japan. Relative economic backwardness and a lack of natural resources suggested export-oriented industrialization as the natural development path. If the country was to pursue this course successfully Japanese goods had to compete in international markets on the basis of both price and quality. This in turn required the importation of western technology and manufacturing know-how. The problem that confronted the Occupation administration and the government was how to pay for technology and capital equipment imports at a time when Japanese manufactures were uncompetitive in international markets.

The solution lay in the adoption of a distinctly nationalistic and quasi-protectionist set of economic policies and administrative procedures.[50] In this way, domestic markets were protected from competition, and the foreign exchange released for technology and capital imports was targeted at improving the productivity and productive potential of industries with good export potential. The two main legislative instruments regulating technology imports were the Foreign Exchange and Foreign Trade Control Law (FEFTCL) of 1949 and the Foreign Investments Law of 1950. Under these laws, technology agreements were only 'validated' once signed off to the satisfaction of the Bank of Japan, the Ministry of Finance, MITI and the Science and Technology Agency.[51] The guiding principle according to a team of British businessmen visiting Japan in 1962 was that agreements should contribute to 'the self-support and sound development of the Japanese economy' and 'the improvement of the international balance of payments'. The system allowed MITI to achieve a high degree of administrative coordination in trying and testing technologies before approving their adoption on an industry-wide basis.[52] In a typical year during the 1950s, more than 100 agreements were signed granting access to foreign technology and patents in exchange for royalty payments of approximately 3 per cent for technology, 5 per cent for patents and 7 per cent for technology plus patents. By 1961, the cost of technology imports had risen to $111 million.[53]

Japanese electronics firms, staffed by experienced engineers and scientists, had the absorptive capacity to make the most of foreign technology imported at what would prove to be bargain prices. Sony, for instance, gained access to transistor technology in 1953 through its patent contract with Western Electric, and by 1957 had launched the world's first transistor radio. It proved a resounding success in both the domestic and export markets. The Japanese had recognized the strategic importance of transistorized solid-state technology, and by 1960, the vacuum tube was effectively obsolete.[54] What made the transistor revolution particularly significant was that it gave manufacturers the opportunity to miniaturize components and end products, saving on both energy and materials. By the late 1960s, the basic transistor itself had been superseded by the more advanced integrated circuit, which led to major savings through process simplification reduced power consumption. The new industrial field of semiconductor manufacturing and was thereby brought into being in Japan. A remarkable amount of technological knowledge flowed into the country during the 1950s and 1960s, representing a striking example of both tacit and explicit knowledge conversions on an industry-wide scale.[55]

Integral to the process of technological absorption was the introduction and refinement of new manufacturing methods. As with fundamental technologies, however, the majority of these methods originated in the United States. It was in the 1940s and early 1950s that Japanese electronics firms made their commitment to quality as a guiding principle. The lead was taken by the Civil Communications Section (CCS) of the Occupation administration, whose course on modern management methods ran for the first time for two six-week periods in 1949 and 1950.[56] The course stressed the importance of engaging employees in the planning process and aligning their aspirations with long-run organizational goals. A key message was that the customer should define quality, while a lack of commitment to quality equated to an indifferent corporate strategy. Particular emphasis was placed on the role of middle managers as change agents, especially technologists and engineers who were encouraged to aspire to senior managerial positions. The graduates of the pioneering CCS course were active in later years in spreading the influential techniques and messages of American management gurus like Deming, Juran and Drucker. A further important source of ideas was the American technical assistance programme to Japan that ran between 1955 and 1962 at a cost of $12 million. The programme took 3,568 individuals in 345 teams from Japan to study business methods in the United States. More than 100 American management consultants and engineers crossed the Pacific to spread the gospel of productivity and quality within large Japanese firms. At the same time, the Japan Productivity Council was formed to disseminate information on modern management methods throughout Japanese industry. Tiratsoo[57] argues that the technical assistance programme, though long overlooked in the management literature, had a profound impact 'in relation to specific techniques and processes, especially those intrinsic to the discipline of industrial engineering... at the very heart of efficient manufacturing'.

The fusion of technological and manufacturing expertise that resulted from (politically inspired) initiatives taken during the reconstruction era had emerged by the 1960s as a defining feature of the Japanese electronics industry. It made possible the rapid commercial deployment of technologies by reducing the lead-time between R&D and the launch of products with mass market potential.[58] Radios, monochrome televisions and colour televisions in turn became hit products at home and abroad, and the dawning of the television age swiftly suggested other possibilities. Initially, broadcasting studios were largely American-equipped, but by 1954 Ikegami Tsushinki had signed technical agreements with RCA and EMI, and within four years was producing its own transmission equipment.[59] This was followed during the 1960s, again using US technology, acquired through collaboration with Ampex, by fully transistorized professional broadcasting equipment (VTRs). Within two years of the sale of the first two VTRs in Japan, both Sony and Toshiba had constructed their own prototypes, to be followed by similar versions from other manufacturers. The experience gained in this way, combined with the mastery of miniaturization, is fundamental to any explanation of Japan's command of the world VTR market by the end of the 1970s.[60]

Mastery of the art of conceiving and manufacturing high-quality products at low cost that appealed to consumers and industrial customers in markets across the world triggered the virtuous circle of growth that saw the Japanese electronics industry go from strength to strength down to the 1990s. Market domination yielded strong cash flows, and because employees and shareholders were modest in their demands, there were exceptional amounts of free cash available for investment. This was targeted at product development, the acquisition and discovery of technological knowledge, investment in new plant and equipment, manufacturing and marketing systems development, and raising the productivity of employees through education and training. Multiple advantages accrued: notably, higher productivity, reduced unit costs, improved quality, more attractive and higher performing products, and short development times. All this worked to consolidate the position of Japanese firms within existing markets and to cultivate and command fresh markets. The sheer dynamic force of the process made for high and sustained rates of industrial growth.[61] Meanwhile, the prospective threats to the system that loomed large from time to time did not materialize. Nations disillusioned by Japanese trading practices felt unable to retaliate or were assuaged when Japanese firms made sizeable direct investments in the United States and Europe.[62] Employees remained compliant and kept faith with a system that delivered security and steadily rising incomes. Shareholders had little to reason to complain about low dividends when the value of their holdings seemed to move forever upwards. Only with the bursting of the bubble economy in 1990 was the Japanese system of corporate governance seriously called into question.[63]

The possession of a regular and lavish supply of investment funds enabled Japanese electronics firms progressively to enhance their technological capabilities.[64] This was done in two distinct but complementary ways. The first was to invest in people and the development of an innovation-minded corporate community. At the heart of this community were university-educated engineers and scientists. In the 1940s and 1950s, these people were in short supply, and in 1959, Japanese electronics firms had only half the number per thousand employees as their US rivals (31 compared to 60).[65] Engineers and scientists were a scarce resource and this fact had an important conditioning effect on national, corporate and functional business strategies. At the national level, the knowledge sharing initiatives supported and guided by MITI were intended to get the most out of a relatively small engineering and scientific workforce. At the corporate level, every effort was made to lure individuals away from universities and other competing employers through the provision of excellent facilities and conditions of employment. Companies offered continuous employment, good rewards and high professional status, and opportunities for personal development at home and in the United States as inducements to join their 'family'.[66] At the functional level, engineers and scientists had of necessity to be 'spread' across the organization, moving periodically between central laboratories and divisions, between R&D and production, and between specific projects and regular operations. They also had need to relate closely to shop-floor workers and to draw upon them for ideas and support.[67] Flexibility and cooperative working were thus born out of necessity.

In our view, three of the defining elements of the Japanese approach to technology acquisition and management were in origin a product of relative economic backwardness. When the electronics industry began to power upward towards the end of the 1950s and when large amounts of free cash became available, familiar norms, standards and methods of working had already been established throughout the electronics industry. These are manifest in what Lazonick and West define as 'organizational integration'.[68] Japanese capitalism is portrayed by them as 'collective', characterized by highly relational communities that extend beyond the boundaries of individual firms, universities or public bodies. Under these social arrangements, 'know-who' is as important as 'know-how' and innovation is frequently the product of multi-disciplinary project teams. R&D and manufacturing are linked through the collective knowledge of engineers and scientists and a common sense of organizational purpose. Ideas are drawn from multiple sources from within and outside firms, and they are developed collectively through the vehicle of the project team.[69] Stability and continuity result from the fact that senior technologists remain with the same firm rather than moving periodically to advance their careers as in the United States. All this continues to apply, even though the initial problem of a lack of graduate engineers and scientists has long since disappeared. Already by the end of the 1970s, the number of people graduating from university with first and higher degrees in electrical and electronic engineering was higher in Japan than in the United States (21,435 against 16,093 in 1979).[70] Moreover, with 80 per cent of R&D concentrated in private firms and directed at civilian ends, Japanese electronics enterprises had moved from a position of critical human resource scarcity to one of abundance.[71]

The second means of enhancing technological capabilities was through the creation and regular enhancement of R&D facilities, systems and routines. Okimoto and Nishi[72] have provided a stylized description of the pyramidal research infrastructure of the large integrated semiconductor manufacturers, and the same description might be applied to the integrated electronics majors. A Central Research Laboratory (CRL) forms the apex, Divisional Laboratories (DLs) occupy the middle levels and a multiplicity of Factory Engineering Laboratories (FELs) forms the baseline. The CRL, operating on a five to ten year timescale, is responsible for nurturing and expanding the fundamental and theoretical technological knowledge of the firm. The DLs are engaged in product development. Interactions with the CRL are two-way: at times, they respond to product ideas pushed downwards; at other times, they commission fundamental research. The FELs take responsibility for the implementation and refinement of manufacturing processes working in close conjunction with relevant DLs and on occasion with central manufacturing process teams. The pyramidal model had its origins in American industry and dates back to the early 1900s. Japanese firms from the late 1950s emulated it: many of the largest CRLs of today (Sony, for example) date from the early 1960s.[73]

In moving from knowledge dependence to knowledge creation, it is not structures and systems *per se* that have served the Japanese electronics industry so well: it is the way in which they have functioned at a human level and have constantly adapted to environmental changes and competitive pressures.[74] The case of Sharp is illustrative.[75] In 1970, Sharp began to develop a new CRL, its Advanced Development and Planning Centre, on a 55-acre greenfield site. The complex took ten years to complete at a cost of Y7.5bn, a sum equivalent to 70 per cent of the company's capitalisation in 1980. The Sharp CRL consists of numerous fundamental R&D groups. Research is commissioned by DLs responsible for product development. Primacy rests at the DL level because it is the divisions that are best placed to anticipate customer requirements. A Production Technology Group is responsible for ensuring on an interactive call and response basis the transfer of technology between corporate R&D and manufacturing. Research and engineering personnel work across the system and are often conscripted to project teams to research a new technology or develop a new product or solve a manufacturing problem. The unifying strategic idea is that of the base technology. Starting from a single base technology (or core component) as many commercial applications as possible are developed (this is known as the 'spiral system'). For example, on the basis of its command of liquid crystal technology, Sharp has 'spiraled out' numerous devices in the fields of home appliances, electronic advertisements, AV equipment, games consoles, medical electronics, industrial sensors, automotive devices, computer screens and many others.

Many Japanese electronics firms have followed a similar path to that of Sharp.[76] The overall thrust has been to evolve, step by step from the disjointed and resource deficient organizations of the 1950s to the highly integrated and well-resourced organizations of today.[77] In the immediate postwar decade, Japanese firms lacked the know-how and systems needed to bring home-grown inventions like the Esaki diode (1957) to commercial fruition. But this situation did not last long. By the 1960s, many firms had the capacity to absorb and make the most of imported technologies. As the industry boomed, the demand for technology from overseas grew rather than receded as the absorptive capacity of firms increased. At the same time, Japanese firms began to invest heavily in more fundamental research, creating an indigenous capability to generate and exploit original ideas. This was signalled by a steep rise in patents issued to Japanese inventors at home and abroad (from 8.9 to 17.9 per cent of all US patents issued between 1975 and 1985).[78] By the early 1980s, it was evident that in non-military electronics, Japan had virtually closed the technology gap with the United States. The Japanese triumph in VLSI, which saw its manufacturers claim 48 per cent of the world semiconductor market in 1987 (compared to 39 per cent for the United States), marked a watershed.[79] Thereafter, it was no longer possible simply to dismiss Japanese firms as technological followers riding on the back of pioneering US corporations: the one-time follower had plainly emerged as a technological leader.

5 Conclusion: Interpretation, Outcomes and Implications

The thrust of the argument put forward in this article is that the technological advance of the Japanese electronics industry (1945–95) was in essence a *product not a primary cause* of industrial growth. We have demonstrated that the industry's surge forward resulted from the interaction of a unique combination of political, economic and cultural forces. Business leaders took full advantage by investing on a massive scale in physical, organizational, human and technological resources. It was success in the marketplace and strong cash flows that allowed Japanese firms to import technology on a large scale, invest in scientists and engineers, and progressively develop world class technological capabilities. This is not to say that technological progress was not essential to industrial growth. Plainly it was. But the movement from knowledge dependence to knowledge creation ultimately followed in the wake of business expansion: technology, down to the 1980s, was a lagging rather than a leading variable in a dynamic process of systemic growth.

Interpretation

Three related theoretical ideas are helpful to a general understanding of the postwar growth and technological advance of the Japanese electronics industry. The first is that of *relative economic backwardness.* According to Gerschenkron,[80] a moderately backward industrializing nation such as Japan in the late 1940s and 1950s would, with strategic guidance from the state and big business, focus its efforts on modernization in a limited number of industries. In such countries, market mechanisms are imperfect and the resources needed for development are in short supply; hence, the drive to concentrate resources and the concomitant internalization of market functions by firms. Corporate and industrial leaders in effect find substitutes for mechanisms and resources that are more readily available in advanced economies. In the case of Japanese electronics, one of the main prerequisites for growth was the acquisition, absorption and deployment of western technologies. The main constraints were financial and human. Industry-wide sharing of (costly) knowledge through MITI and trade associations, the concentration of (scarce) engineering and scientific talent in private sector enterprises and rotational methods of deploying technologists, may be seen as strategic responses to the exigencies of moderate economic backwardness.

The important point is that economic backwardness fundamentally conditioned the development of the Japanese electronics industry. In terms of our second theoretical idea, its pattern of growth was *path dependent*: heavily influenced by systems, routines and norms established at an early stage.[81] Administrative coordination through MITI and trade associations proved to be efficacious in the diffusion of technology and management techniques. Likewise, the concentration of R&D in private sector firms soon became structurally embedded. Meanwhile, at the operational level, many of the working practices that were born of necessity, such as the rotation of technologists and the extensive use of project teams, were culturally and systemically assimilated. History casts a long shadow.

We argue that the movement from knowledge dependence to knowledge creation was gradual, and resist the idea of staged paradigmatic shifts. The construct that best embraces our view of the change process is Lazonick and West's *organizational integration hypothesis*,[82] the third of our key theoretical ideas. In the Gerschenkron model, economic backwardness is equated with variability, disjointedness and a lack of integration at the corporate, industrial and national levels. These were certainly features of the Japanese electronics industry immediately after the war. The trajectory was towards the integration of structures, systems and processes in the quest for higher levels of organizational effectiveness and efficiency. Integration extended beyond individual firms backward to suppliers and forward to customers. Conventional distinctions between R&D and manufacturing became blurred.[83] Thus, while path dependency may impose constraints, it simultaneously embraces beneficial tendencies. In Japan, the tendency was towards organizational integration and the creation of deep-seated organizational and technological capabilities. Japanese electronics firms were thereby able to progress more rapidly than their American rivals, eventually emerging at the forefront of the non-military world electronics industry.

Outcomes and Implications

Fransman, in analyzing the characteristics of the Japanese 'technology-creating system', draws attention, as we have done, to the importance of history in fashioning its development. In his view, the crucial role played by MITI and state-funded laboratories was in reducing levels of uncertainty in private firms with regard to investment in R&D. By identifying and part-funding future-oriented research programmes, especially in industrial electronics, creative partnerships were formed and leading-edge technological knowledge disseminated throughout the industry. Economies of scale and scope in R&D were secured in the process. In this way, the state was able to lend strategic direction to the industry without destroying the benefits of competition between firms in various application domains. The industry was thus able to move successfully, as the technology gap between the United States and Japan was closed, from the development of 'technology for tomorrow' to the creation of 'technology for the day after tomorrow'.[84]

This aspect of the transition from knowledge dependence to knowledge creation is consistent with the thesis presented in this article. Japanese firms, when confronted by the problems resulting from economic backwardness, needed support and direction from the state in order to compensate for the high incidence of 'market failure'. The internalization of activities and routines was a second consequence, contributing to the creation of a distinctive system of corporate governance. Electronics enterprises became highly vertically integrated and affiliated in family groups. The dominant firms at the hub of the Japanese industry were resistant to voluntary collaboration in R&D because, as Fransman points out, the transaction costs of policing agreements were too high.[85] Only with state aid could transaction costs be reduced to an acceptable level. When seen in this light, the technological history of the Japanese electronics industry is Janus-faced: at once a united national endeavour and a struggle between individual firms for the control of key technologies.

What is true today was just as true in the immediate postwar years. The corporate struggle focused then on the race to acquire foreign technology, with MITI and other government agencies mediating in pursuit of the collective good. Long after Japanese firms had begun to make independent technological advances, they continued to import far more technology than they exported.[86] But the persistence of a negative balance of trade in technology, far from being a sign of continued backwardness, was a reflection of a deliberate strategy: the big players in the industry sought to extract the best technology they could from the rest of the world while limiting access to that which was 'made in Japan'. This is entirely consistent with the policy of 'internalize and control' that has long been a defining feature of the industry. The current technology policies of Japanese firms bear testimony to the enduring nature of this characteristic logic-of-action.[87] Within Japan, electronics firms occupied second, third, fourth, fifth, seventh and ninth positions in the national R&D expenditure league table in 1996. Outside Japan, they have become senior partners in numerous global R&D networks, embracing private sector firms and top research universities.[88] There is nothing fanciful about such collaborations: the aim, as ever, is to gain control over scientific and engineering knowledge that can be integrated within the technology-creating systems of Japanese firms.[89] What is certain is that Japan has learned the lesson of its own history: its intellectual property will never be so freely dissipated as that of the United States when it was the undisputed leader of the world electronics industry.

Notes

1 The authors would like to thank Reed Charity for funding our research. The article has benefited from the comments of two anonymous referees and participants in the Technology and Globalisation stream of the Asia Pacific Researchers in Organization Studies (APROS) conference, Sydney, December 2000.
2 M. Lewis, R. Fitzgerald & C. Harvey, *The Growth of Nations: Culture, Competitiveness and the Problem of Globalization* (Bristol, 1996), pp. 55–110.
3 A. Maddison, 'Macroeconomic accounts for European countries' in B. Van Ark & N. Crafts (eds), *Quantitative Aspects of Post-war European Economic Growth* (Cambridge, 1996), p. 32.
4 K. Sato, 'Saving and Investment' in K. Yamamura & Y. Yasuba (eds), *The Political Economy of Japan: Vol. 1 The Domestic Transformation* (Stanford, 1987).
5 A. Maddison, *Explaining the Economic Performance of Nations* (Cheltenham, 1995).
6 Electronics Industries Association of Japan, *Facts and Figures* (Tokyo, 1993).
7 A. Jaffar, 'Japanese Electronics Multinationals in Malaysia: A Value Added Analysis of Strategy and Industry Structure' (University of London Ph.D., 1998). Jaffar estimates labour's share of valued added at 44 per cent in 1983 compared to 57 per cent ten years later. Comparable figures are not available for earlier years, but it is nonetheless plain that well before the mid-1980s Japanese electronics manufacturers had very large amounts of cash available for reinvestment.
8 J. Price, *Japan Works: Power and Politics in Postwar Industrial Relations* (Ithaca, 1997), pp. 270–73.
9 E. F. Denison & W. K. Chung, How *Japan's Economy Grew So Fast: The Sources of Postwar Expansion* (Washington DC, 1976).
10 V. Argy & L. Stein, *The Japanese Economy* (Basingstoke, 1997).
11 R. Komiya & M. Itoh, 'International Trade and Industrial Policy' in T. Inoguchi & D. I. Okimoto (eds), *The Political Economy of Japan: Vol. 2 The Changing International Context* (Stanford, 1988).
12 R. Steven, *Japan and the New World Order: Global Investments, Trade and Finance* (Basingstoke, 1996).
13 M. Shinohara, *Industrial Growth, Trade and Dynamic Patterns in the Japanese Economy* (Tokyo, 1982).
14 K. Imai, 'The Japanese Pattern of Innovation and its Evolution' in N. Rosenberg, R. Landau & D. C. Mowery (eds), *Technology and the Wealth of Nations* (Stanford, 1992).
15 A. D. Chandler, *Scale and Scope: The Dynamics of Industrial Capitalism* (Cambridge Mass., 1990).
16 S. Harryson, *Japanese Technology and Innovation Management* (Cheltenham, 1998); W. M. Fruin, *The Japanese Enterprise System: Competitive Strategies and Cooperative Structures* (Oxford, 1992); W. M. Fruin, *Knowledge Works: Managing Intellectual Capital at Toshiba* (Oxford, 1997).
17 C. J. McMillan, *The Japanese Industrial System* (Berlin, 1985).
18 T. Fujino, *Globalisation and Consolidated Management* (Tokyo, 1998).
19 M. E. Porter, *The Competitive Advantage of Nations* (Basingstoke, 1990).

20 Lewis, Fitzgerald & Harvey, *The Growth of Nations*, pp. 1–54.
21 W. K. Tabb, *The Postwar Japanese System: Cultural Economy and Economic Transformation* (Oxford, 1995).
22 H. Morikawa, 'The Role of the Managerial Enterprise in Japan's Economic Growth: Focus on the 1950s', *Business History*, 37 (1995), pp. 32–45.
23 T. Nakamura, *The Postwar Japanese Economy: Its Development and Structure* (Tokyo, 1995), pp. 150–55.
24 M. Morishima, *Why Has Japan 'Succeeded'?* (Cambridge, 1982), pp. 164–65.
25 Y. Kosai, *The Era of High-speed Growth: Notes on the Postwar Japanese Economy* (Tokyo, 1986).
26 On 15 August 1971, after repeated efforts to persuade Japan seriously to contemplate policies aimed at reducing a worsening US balance of payments situation, President Nixon unilaterally announced a temporary surcharge of 10 per cent on imports. Under the terms of the subsequent Smithsonian Agreement of 18 December 1971, the surcharge was scrapped and a realignment of the major exchange rate parities was inaugurated, in effect paving the way for an era of floating currencies.
27 R. Belderbos, *Japanese Electronics Multinationals and Strategic Trade Policies* (Oxford, 1997).
28 J. Price, *Japan Works: Power and Paradox in Postwar Industrial Relations* (Ithaca, 1997); A. Gordon, *The Evolution of Labor Relations in Japan: Heavy Industries, 1853–1955* (Cambridge Mass., 1988).
29 S. Sugayama, 'Work Rules, Wages and Single Status: The Shaping of the Japanese Employment System', *Business History*, 37 (1995), pp. 120–40.
30 Y. Suzuki, *Japanese Management Structures 1920–80* (Basingstoke, 1991).
31 J. Abegglen & G. Stalk, *Kaisha: The Japanese Corporation* (New York, 1985).
32 Fruin, *The Japanese Enterprise System*.
33 J. Tidd, J. Bessant & K. Pavitt, *Managing Innovation: Integrating Technological, Market and Organisational Change* (Chichester, 1997), pp. 85–87.
34 C. J. McMillan, 'The State as Economic Engine: Lessons from the Japanese Experience', appeared in *Journal of Far Eastern Business* (now known as *Asia Pacific Business Review*) Vol. 1 No. 3 Spring 1995, pp. 1–16; C. Johnson, *MITI and the Japanese Miracle* (Stanford, 1982); M. Aoki, 'Unintended Fit: Organizational Evolution and Government Design of Institutions in Japan' in M. Aoki, H-K. Kim & M. Okuno-Fujiwara (eds), *The Role of Government in East Asian Economic Development* (Oxford, 1997); M. J. Scher, *Japanese Interfirm Networks and Their Main Banks* (Basingstoke, 1997); B. Johnstone, *We were Burning: Japanese Entrepreneurs and the Forging of the Electronic Age* (New York, 1999); W. Lazonick, 'The Japanese Economy and Corporate Reform: What Path to Sustainable Prosperity', *Industrial and Corporate Change*, 8 (1999), pp. 607–633.
35 Chandler, *Scale and Scope*.
36 H. Morikawa, 'Japan: Increasing Organizational Capabilities of Large Industrial Enterprises, 1880s–1980s' in A. D. Chandler, F. Amatori & T. Hikino, *Big Business and the Wealth of Nations* (Cambridge, 1997).
37 H. Odagiri, *Growth though Competition, Competition through Growth: Strategic Management and the Economy in Japan* (Oxford, 1992).
38 Bureau of Statistics, Office of the Prime Minister, *Japan Statistical Yearbook* (Tokyo, annual volumes, 1948–60).

39 Y. Kimura, *The Japanese Semiconductor Industry: Structure, Competitive Strategies and Performance* (Greenwich Conn., 1984).
40 Jaffar, *Japanese Electronics Multinationals.*
41 D. E. Westney, 'The Evolution of Japan's Industrial Research and Development' in M. Aoki & R. Dore (eds), *The Japanese Firm: Sources of Competitive Strength* (Oxford, 1994).
42 M. Kikuchi, 'Cooperation in Japan with Higher Education' in G. O. Phillips, *Innovation and Technology Transfer in Japan and Europe* (London, 1989).
43 K. Oshima, 'The High Technology Gap: A View from Japan' in A. J. Pierre, *A High Technology Gap: Europe, American and Japan* (New York, 1987).
44 H. Odagiri & H. Goto, *Technology and Industrial Policy in Japan: Building Capabilities by Learning, Innovation and Public Policy* (Oxford, 1996); T. Morris-Suzuki, *The Technological Transformation of Japan* (Cambridge, 1995).
45 F. Kodama, *Analyzing Japanese High Technologies: The Techno Paradigm Shift* (London, 1991).
46 T. Okazaki, 'The Japanese Firm under the Wartime Planned Economy' in Aoki & Dore, *The Japanese Firm.*
47 S. Nakayama, *Science, Technology and Society in Postwar Japan* (London, 1991).
48 W. M. Fransman, *The Market and Beyond: Information Technology in Japan* (Cambridge, 1990), p. 13: 'The rapidity with which transistor and computer technologies were acquired from the United States and Europe and reproduced in Japan was largely a function of the substantial capabilities that had been built up in the country since the 1920s... Although the technological capabilities of these industries still lagged behind those of the world's leaders by the 1950s, enough had been learned to facilitate a fast and successful assimilation of the cluster of new technologies that heralded the arrival of the information age'.
49 T. Hayashi, *The Japanese Experience in Technology: From Transfer to Self-Reliance* (Tokyo, 1990).
50 W. R. Nester, *Japanese Industrial Targeting: The Neomercantilist Path to Economic Superpower* (Basingstoke, 1991); J.-S. Shin, *The Economics of Latecomers: Catching-up, Technology Transfer and Institutions in Germany, Japan and South Korea* (London, 1996).
51 Kosai, *The Era of High-speed Growth*, p. 55.
52 J. G. Montalvo & Y. Yafeh, 'A Microeconometric Analysis of Technology Transfer: The Case of Licensing Agreements of Japanese Firms', *International Journal of Industrial Organization*, 12 (1994), pp. 227–44.
53 Economic Planning Agency, *Economic Survey of Japan* (Tokyo, 1962), p. 59.
54 Odagiri & Goto, *Technology and Industrial Policy in Japan.*
55 I. Nonaka & H. Takeuchi, *The Knowledge-Creating Company: How Japanese Companies Create the Dynamics of Innovation* (Oxford, 1995).
56 In researching the activities of the CCS, we had the benefit of an extended interview with one of its leading lights, Homer Sarasohn, conducted in London by Tony Hayward on 13 December 1995. Matsushita reprinted the CCS course textbook in 1995 under the title *Management Manual.* Further reflections on the CCS and the origins of the quality movement in Japan derive from Y. Kondo, 'The Japanese Experience of Quality in the

Last Half Century', presentation in London 13 December 1995. Professor Kondo is a winner of the Deming Prize, and since 1970, he has been a council member of the Union of Japanese Scientists and Engineers (more familiarly known as JUSE).

57 N. Tiratsoo, 'The United States Technical Assistance Programme in Japan, 1955–62', *Business History*, 42 (2000).

58 W. M. Fruin, 'Competing in the Old-Fashioned Way: Localising and Integrating Knowledge Resources in Fast-to-Market Competition' in J. K. Liker, J. Ettlie & J. C. Campbell (eds), *Engineered in Japan: Japanese Technology Practices* (Oxford, 1995).

59 Ikegami Tsushinki Co., *Company Profile* (Tokyo, 1992).

60 Harryson, *Japanese Technology and Innovation Management*, pp. 126–49.

61 D. J. Teece, G. Pisano & A. Shuen, 'Dynamic Capabilities and Strategic Management', *Strategic Management Journal*, 18 (1997), pp. 509–34.

62 Belberados, *Japanese Electronics Multinationals*; Y. Kimura, 'Japanese Direct Investment in the European Semiconductor Industry' in N. Mason & D. Encarnation (eds), *Does Ownership Matter? Japanese Multinationals in Europe* (Oxford, 1994).

63 W. Lazonick, 'The Japanese Economy and Corporate Reform'; R. P. Dore, 'The Asian Form of Capitalism' in P. H. Admiraal (ed.), *The Corporate Triangle: The Structure and Performance of Corporate Systems in the Global Economy* (Oxford, 1997); R. Bostock & C. Stoney, 'Japanese Corporate Governance: Governance for the Twenty-First Century or a Model in Decline?', *Asia Pacific Business Review*, 4 (1997), pp. 63–82.

64 J. Vestal, *Industrial Policy and Japanese Industrial Development 1945–1990* (Oxford, 1993).

65 C. Freeman, *Technology Policy and Economic Performance: Lessons from Japan* (London, 1987), p. 10.

66 H. Itoh, 'Japanese Human Resource Management from the Viewpoint of Incentive Theory' in Aoki & Dore, *The Japanese Firm*.

67 D. M. Schroder & A. G. Robinson, 'Training, Continuous Improvement and Human Relations: The US TWI Programs and Japanese Management Style', *California Management Review*, 35 (1993), pp. 35–57.

68 W. Lazonick & J. West, 'Organizational Integration and Competitive Advantage: Explaining Strategy and Performance in American Industry' in G. Dosi, D. J. Teece & J. Chytry (eds), *Technology, Organization and Competitiveness: Perspectives in Industrial and Corporate Change* (Oxford, 1998).

69 K. Imai & K. B. Clark, 'Integration and Dynamic Capability: Evidence from Product Development and Mainframe Computers', *Industrial and Corporate Change*, 3 (1994), pp. 557–605.

70 Freeman, *Technology Policy and Economic Performance*, p. 47.

71 Freeman, *Technology Policy and Economic Performance*, p. 11.

72 D. I. Okimoto & Y. Nishi, 'R&D Organisation in Japanese and American Semiconductor Firms' in Aoki & Dore, *The Japanese Firm*.

73 Nakayama, Science, *Technology and Policy in Postwar Japan*, pp. 97–102; M. Kenney & R. Florida, 'The organization and geography of Japanese R&D: results from a survey of Japanese electronics and biotechnology firms', *Research Policy*, 23 (1994), pp. 305–23.

74 M. Fransman, *Japan's Computer and Communications Industry: The Evolution of Global Giants and Global Competitiveness* (Oxford, 1995).

75 Tony Hayward compiled the case study material on Sharp. This consists of in-house documents on technology development and management, field notes and interview transcripts. Interviews were held with R&D personnel at the Tenri and Makuhari research facilities in May 1997. A further interview was conducted in Oxford with Dr Clive Bradley, then managing director of Sharp Laboratories Europe, in November 1996.

76 Fruin, *Knowledge Works*; S. Collinson & A. Molina, *Reorganizing for Knowledge Integration and Constituency Building in the Age of Multimedia: Product Development at Philips and Sony* (JETS paper no. 12) (Edinburgh, 1995); Harryson, *Japanese Technology and Innovation Management.*

77 J. Sigurdson, *Science and Technology in Japan*, 3rd edn (London, 1995).

78 Freeman, *Technology Policy and Economic Performance*, p. 21.

79 T. Forester, *Silicon Samurai: How Japan Conquered the World's IT Industry* (Oxford, 1993), p. 45.

80 A. Gerschenkron, *Economic Backwardness in Historical Perspective* (Cambridge Mass., 1962).

81 D. M. Mueller, 'First-Mover Advantages and Path Dependence', *International Journal of Industrial Organization*, 15 (1997), pp. 827–50.

82 Lazonick and West, 'Organizational Integration and Competitive Advantage'.

83 Imai & Clark, 'Integration and Dynamic Capability'.

84 Fransman, *The Market and Beyond*, pp. 256–76.

85 Fransman, *The Market and Beyond*, pp. 266–76.

86 Japan's overall technology trade (import and export of patents, designs, technology transfers, trademarks and software licenses) with the rest of the world was broadly in balance by 1990. The balance of trade with the United States remained overwhelmingly in favour of the United States: accounting for about 30 per cent of Japan's technology exports and 70 per cent of imports at the end of our period (1945–95). In 1996, the deficit with the United States stood at Y120bn. It ought, however, to be noted that the gap closed significantly during the 1990s according to the Agency of Industrial Science and Technology, *Trends in Principal Indicators of Research and Development Activities in Japan* (Tokyo, 1998), pp. 48–57.

87 J. A. Ordover, 'A Patent System for Both Diffusion and Exclusion', *Journal of Economic Perspectives*, 5 (1991), pp. 43–60; Y. Okada & S. Asaba, 'The Patent System in Japan' in A. Goto & H. Odagiri (eds), *Innovation in Japan* (Oxford, 1997).

88 D. Cairncross, 'The Strategic Role of Japanese R&D Centres in the UK' in N. Campbell & F. Burton, *Japanese Multinationals: Strategies and Management in the Global Kaisha* (London, 1994); L. Turner, D. Ray & A. Hayward, *The British Research of Japanese Companies* (London, 1997); H. Odagiri & H. Yasuda, 'Overseas Activities of Japanese Firms' in Goto & Odagiri, *Innovation in Japan.*

89 Y. Teramoto *et al.*, 'Global Strategy in the Japanese Semiconductor Industry: Knowledge Creation through Strategic Alliances' in Campbell & Burton, *Japanese Multinationals*; K. Imai, 'Globalization and Cross-Border Networks in Japanese Firms' in T. Anderson (ed.), *Japan: A European Perspective* (Basingstoke, 1993).

Retrospective

Charles Harvey and Mairi Maclean

It is two decades since we published our article on the industrial growth and technological advance of the Japanese electronics industry in the *Journal of Industrial History* (Harvey, Hayward & Maclean, 2001a). Time has been called a 'mighty sculptor' (Yourcenar, 1992), and being given the opportunity to reflect back on this study after the passage of so much time has been an interesting, and poignant, exercise.

It has proved interesting, because at the time of writing 20 years ago, Japan had become established as a global electronics powerhouse with a commanding presence in each of the three main markets: consumer, industrial and components. This article stemmed from Tony Hayward's doctoral research and sought to explain how Japanese firms had transitioned from technological laggards in 1945 to technological leaders 50 years later. Under the twin influences of Porter's (1990) macro study of *The Competitive Advantage of Nations* and Teece, Pisano and Shuen's (1997) micro exploration of dynamic capabilities, we put forward a comprehensive macro–micro explanation of Japanese success in developing and exploiting solid state electronics technologies. This entailed close statistical work to demarcate eras and compute rates of growth in different sectors of the industry and synthesizing the work of numerous other scholars such as Fransman (1995), Nakamura (1995), Nonaka and Takeuchi (1995), Odagiri and Goto (1996) and Fruin (1997). Our original insights stemmed mainly from corporate case studies based on company documents and interviews with executives and US officials involved in the transfer of technologies and managerial knowledge to Japan in the 1950s. Two main conclusions emerged. First, the deepening of technological and organizational capabilities in Japan *followed* from market success and the abundant free cash this generated. Second, the process of deepening technological capabilities was one based initially on *creative imitation and adaptation* and then on *continuous improvement* rather than on disruptive innovations (Harvey, Hayward & Maclean, 2001a, 2001b).

These findings hold up well and are consistent with subsequent research and current thinking on technological change and innovation (Arthur, 2009; Nonaka & Takeuchi, 2019). We continue to believe that our interpretation in all essential aspects is sound. Moreover, what has become evident in recent years is that our observation that in the case of Japanese electronics technological deepening was driven by market success has wider implications for the theory of dynamic capabilities.

Put simply, the pre-existence of advanced technological and organizational capabilities do not alone constitute a dynamic capability, as laggards endowed with compelling cost advantages can transition rapidly from technological laggard to leader, as in electronics, first in Japan and then later in Korea and China. We hold that it is only through *theoretically sensitive historical analysis* that the theory of dynamic capabilities can be rendered more realistic and context sensitive (Suddaby, Coraiola, Harvey & Foster, 2019).

Reflecting on our study has also proved poignant because our co-author, Tony Hayward, is no longer with us. Tony was a larger-than-life character who lived and breathed all things Japanese. He spoke the language fluently, a rarity in those days amongst the British, as now, and had a Japanese wife, Chizoya. Before completing his doctoral studies at Royal Holloway, University of London, under Charles's supervision, he had worked as a roadie for Eric Clapton, with whom he had formed a good relationship, and who had given him the corner of his estate in Surrey where Tony had built a beautiful Japanese house and garden.

Since completing this research on Japan 20 years ago, our own work has developed in a new direction. Most notably, we have contributed to the burgeoning body of literature that aims to reappraise the place of historical research in organization studies by integrating organizational research with historical approaches and methods (Maclean, Harvey & Clegg, 2016; Maclean, Clegg, Suddaby & Harvey, 2021). This, together with our work on business elites, now forms our principal research area (Maclean, Harvey & Kling, 2014).

It is heartening for us that our joint work on the rise of the Japanese electronics industry, which in many ways was a precursor for our later elaboration of historical organization studies, is being given a new lease of life in the present volume. We are grateful to the editors of the present volume for making this happen. Tony would have been delighted. This chapter is dedicated to him.

References

Arthur, W.B. (2009). *The Nature of Technology: What It Is and How It Evolves*. New York: Free Press.

Fransman, M. (1995). *Japan's Computer and Communications Industry: The Evolution of Global Giants and Global Competitiveness*. Oxford: Oxford University Press.

Fruin, W.M. (1997). *Knowledge Works: Managing Intellectual Capital at Toshiba*. Oxford: Oxford University Press.

Harvey, C., Hayward, T. & Maclean, M. (2001a). From knowledge dependence to knowledge creation: Industrial growth and the technological advance of the Japanese electronics industry. *Journal of Industrial History*, 4(2): 1–23.

Harvey, C., Hayward, T. & Maclean, M. (2001b). Good luck or fine judgement? The growth and development of the Japanese electronics industry, 1945–95. *Asia Pacific Business Review*, 8(1): 102–126.

Maclean, M., Clegg, S.R., Suddaby, R. & Harvey, C. (Eds) (2021). *Historical Organization Studies: Theory and Applications*. London: Routledge.

Maclean, M., Harvey, C. & Clegg, S.R. (2016). Conceptualizing historical organization studies. *Academy of Management Review*, 41(4): 609–632.

Maclean, M., Harvey, C. & Kling, G. (2014). Pathways to power: Class, hyper-agency and the French corporate elite. *Organization Studies*, 35(6): 825–855.

Nakamura, T. (1995). *The Postwar Japanese Economy: Its Development and Structure*. Tokyo: University of Tokyo Press.

Nonaka, I. & Takeuchi, H. (1995). *The Knowledge-Creating Company: How Japanese Companies Create the Dynamics of Innovation*. Oxford: Oxford University Press.

Nonaka, I. & Takeuchi, H. (2019). *The Wise Company: How Companies Create Continuous Innovation*. Oxford: Oxford University Press.

Odagiri, H. & Goto, A. (1996). *Technology and Industrial Policy in Japan: Building Capabilities by Learning, Innovation and Public Policy*. Oxford: Clarendon Press.

Porter, M.E. (1990). *The Competitive Advantage of Nations*. New York: Macmillan.

Suddaby, R., Coraiola, D., Harvey, C. & Foster, W. (2019). History and the micro-foundations of dynamic capabilities. *Strategic Management Journal*, 41(3): 530–556.

Teece, D.J., Pisano, G. & Shuen, A. (1997). Dynamic capabilities and strategic management. *Strategic Management Journal*, 18(7): 509–533.

Yourcenar, M. (1992). *That Mighty Sculptor, Time*. New York: Farrar Straus & Giroux.

Management qualification and dissemination of knowledge in regional innovation systems

The case of Norway 1930s–1990s

Ove Bjarnar, Rolv Petter Amdam and Hallgeir Gammelsæter

Introduction

Within national borders, great variations between different regions have been observed when it comes to innovation and economic development. The character of regional variations has been explored through dimensions like the existence of different models of industrialisation, cultural variations between regions and through the varying importance of regional innovation systems and learning systems.

In recent theories on regional innovation, globalisation challenges in particular make the innovative capacity of firms and regions of strategic importance.[1] Competitive advantage is claimed to be maintained through innovation based on localised processes.[2] Interactive learning and knowledge flowing smoothly between regional actors is therefore seen as a basic provision for processes of innovation.[3] Political intervention in such processes should aim at the systematic promotion of localised learning economies.[4]

According to Lundvall, the concept of innovation system is broadly taken to include 'all parts and aspects of the economic structure and set up affecting learning as well as searching and exploring – the production system, the marketing system and the system of finance present themselves as subsystems in which learning takes place'.[5] Innovation systems have normally been referred to as national systems, but inspired by the political initiatives towards a Europe of regions and economic success stories of territorially agglomerated clusters of SMEs (e.g. the Third Italy), the way economic policies are reformulated at regional levels has attracted greater interest.[6] In this article, the term regional innovation system is borrowed not with the intention to strictly identify, define and discuss the relations between all its parts, but rather to highlight how institutional arrangements designed

DOI: 10.4324/9780429059001

to promote knowledge flows and management education in regional territories must be incorporated within a larger system of relations between governmental, legal, institutional and business actors.

Despite a lot of debate about regional innovation systems and localised as opposed to placeless learning, the role of knowledge flows between higher education and business, particularly to managers in executive positions, is not extensively treated in innovation systems analyses.[7] Lundvall, for example, while strongly emphasising the importance of the interplay between business and education in national innovation systems, does not treat this issue at any sufficient level of concreteness. Likewise, in a recent Norwegian study, the role of the education system is depicted in only general terms.[8] A sharper focus on the flows of management knowledge between business and providers of higher education and training is therefore highly warranted.

The purpose of this article is, by using both a wide historical and contemporary material from Norway, to provide a new and more detailed empirical foundation for discussing the role of dissemination of technical, organisational and managerial knowledge within regional innovation systems. Accordingly, we focus on qualification for management in regional innovation systems. The article is grounded on thorough investigations of central, regional and local archives together with a number of public and semi-public reports and documents. This material is, furthermore, combined with broader survey studies (see Table 1), and also includes recent studies partly based on in-depth interviews with central actors.

Qualification for management in 'regional innovation systems'

If we broadly accept the idea of regional innovation systems, it is important to differentiate between two facets of such systems. On the one hand, such systems include the activities of national (and sometimes international) institutions and companies. On the other, they include actors and institutions that origin from the regional interaction patterns, or has the region as their primary domain.[9] Our position is that the managers of regional business and institutions are key actors in utilising the links between the national and the regional. They are the actors that have access to both levels. The understanding of the systems of flow of knowledge is therefore of importance if we want to understand the territorial dimension of learning and innovation.[10]

The idea of localised as opposed to placeless learning is related to the idea that innovation is primarily the result of interactive learning processes influenced by local economic structures, values, cultures, institutions and histories. If this is correct, regional innovation requires that managers and entrepreneurs possess and utilise local, often tacit knowledge, deriving either from practical work experience or from education and training taking place in a regional context. Management education at the national level do not likely incorporate such territorially defined knowledge. Tacit knowledge and interactive learning have been attached to the so-called associative identity, identity that stems from participation, i.e. that people actually act together in a certain area, activities that are geographically anchored. In this sense, a regional university college, for example, is only *regional* in a deeper meaning if it is associated with activities important *in* and *for* the region. It is therefore not straightforward to disseminate knowledge between small businesses and academic institutions, unless it takes place 'inside' the existing culture, through a *flow of knowledge* between 'partners'. This flow of knowledge depends on the use of 'language', and lecturers and researchers often seem to have other 'language codes' than managers in regional business. For example, managers often have to express themselves in a context-specific code, whereas researchers are trained in using more general abstract codes (context-independent). Accordingly, in order to be able to assist in the application of context-independent abstract economic theories scholars must learn the local context-specific codes. Interactive learning thus depends on the development of arenas where different actors can develop a common language.[11]

It has, however, been emphasised in the literature on regional innovation that regional systems in order to be competitive need to combine local knowledge with knowledge produced at international and national arenas. The inability to combine different kinds of knowledge may create situations where firms are locked in their own constrained world. Thus, the challenge is to create systems that promote the blending of different kinds of knowledge, so that regional systems can produce not only incremental but also radical innovations.[12]

The implication of these ideas of localised learning processes is that regional innovation systems, if viable, incorporate subsystems that enforce both knowledge flows between firms, service producers and R&D institutions, and management education that, on the one hand, equip managers to seek, understand and implement external ideas and concepts, while, on the other, crediting local structures, values, histories, etc. Despite the implications the ideas of regional innovation systems and localised learning have on ideas of knowledge flows and management, there are few if any studies that combine the focus on management knowledge with more in-depth historical analyses of regional systems of innovation. In the following, we intend to describe and assess to what extent different historical 'regimes' have facilitated knowledge flows between managers, educational institutions and other knowledge providers since the 1930s.

Three historical regimes

In Norway, the policy of transferring knowledge to regional business has developed through three different regimes with its respective systemic traits. The term 'systemic' is referring to the fact that actors depend on utilising knowledge from different sources when they innovate. Innovative activity is, subsequently, collective and interactive processes. In order to be systemic, however, these learning processes must be attached to institutions on national or regional level, or at least connected to clusters.[13]

The first regime was active from 1917 until 1953, based on the co-operation between small business advisory branches in the regions, *Småindustrikontorer* (SIK), and a semi-public advisory organisation *Statens teknologiske institutt* (STI), which was set up in 1916 in order to facilitate flow of knowledge to businesses by the use of liaisons or consultants. The most important feature of the regime was its ability to convey knowledge to entrepreneurs.

The second regime emerged in 1953, as *Norsk Produktivitetsinstitutt* (the Norwegian Productivity Institute or (NPI)), was created in connection with the Marshall Plan and the productivity drive in Europe. The NPI established close relations to the STI, and promoted dissemination of knowledge to regional networks of companies. Through the involvement of the NPI, the scope of the knowledge dissemination was widened to include international knowledge to a new extent, and the dissemination system was increasingly designed to embrace regional businesses. Through lasting knowledge networks and series of meetings involving experts and local managers, regional arenas emerged which stimulated localised learning. The most striking characteristic of the system was its capability to disseminate knowledge through networking between businesses, and between businesses and knowledge producers.

The third regime emerged after 1987, as the Government decided that the County authorities should take over the local branches of the STI and be responsible for developing the regional flow of knowledge. The STI was, accordingly, dissolved, and a county driven organisation was set up in its place. This move was motivated by a new knowledge-based paradigm for innovation and economic development in the

Norwegian industrial and regional policy, gaining strength from the beginning of the 1980s. It emphasised the interaction *inside* the region between business and new academic institutions, Regional University Colleges (RCs), set up in the regions from the 1970s. Furthermore, regional businesses were exposed to a growing number of governmental development programmes, partly aimed at strengthening the interaction between regional partners. The most important feature of the new system was, accordingly, dissemination of knowledge through public intervention programmes.

However, the networking tradition of the previous phase was now challenged, and we argue that the new system did not meet the expectations of vitalising the regional dissemination system. Instead of strengthening existing regional arenas for local managers, the innovation system has become more intransparent. Furthermore, the RCs failed in graduating students from the regions to functions of top management in regional business, and despite many efforts, ambitions to integrate formal education into the dissemination network yielded only poor results. The RCs developed into academic institutions whereas the dissemination network was impaired when key institutions like NPI and STI were either dissolved or structurally disintegrated.

Much of the illustrative empirical material is taken from the Møre and Romsdal region in West Norway. The region is rich on historical evidences that have been utilised in research on the productivity drive in post-war Norway and the dissemination of internationally and nationally produced knowledge to and inside the region.[14] The region, moreover, has been described historically as a successful example of a regional system of innovation, although current research tends to downplay its innovative character.[15]

The Møre and Romsdal region (see Map 1) occupied only a peripheral position during the industrial breakthrough in Norway around 1900. However, from the 1920s, small-scale manufacturing industry (especially furniture, textile and small shipyards) developed rapidly. When the Norwegian heavy industry in the 1920s and 1930s suffered from crises, this new small-scale industry developed well, and contributed to restructuring the Norwegian manufacturing industry, which changed dramatically from being dominated by an export oriented industry to a small-scale industry producing for the domestic market. While 27.2 per cent of all employees in manufacturing industry in Norway worked in small companies with less than 50 employees in 1930, 41.9 per cent worked in such small companies in 1948. Møre and Romsdal county became one of the centres of this new small-scale industry. While the more heavily industrialised parts of Southern and Eastern Norway experienced a dramatic period of downsizing and deindustrialisation from the mid-1970s, the manufacturing industry in Møre and Romsdal kept its position. During the period from 1967 to 1975 Norwegian shipyards in general became more specialised and larger. As a consequence, several shipyards lost their flexibility and did not manage to adjust to new products during the years of crises from the mid-1970s. The shipbuilding industry in Møre and Romsdal, however, specialised in building small ships and in repairing old ships.

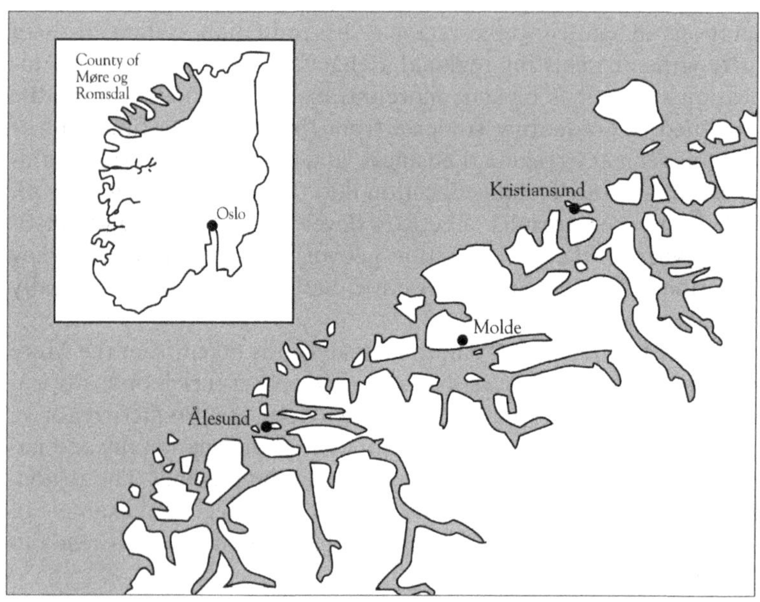

Population development 1900–2000

	1900	1950	1975	2000
Kristiansund	13,500	16,400	23,100	22,100
Molde	5,300	11,700	20,300	23,700
Alesund	15,900	27,200	34,800	38,900
County total	136,100	191,600	231,100	243,200
County/country	6.1%	5.8%	5.8%	5.4%

The city borders have changed through the period. The population numbers are therefore calculated for the cities and specific areas round them.
Sources: Statistics Norway, Censuses and Statistic Yearbook/Regional Statistics.

Map 2.1 The Møre and Romsdal region.

In this way, the district combined growth with an old flexible production form. During the period of crises from the mid-1970s, these shipyards adjusted better to the new market situation than was the case in other parts of Norway. As a result, Møre and Romsdal strengthened its position as a centre of shipbuilding in Norway during the 1980s and 1990s. Furthermore, while the number of employees within the manufacturing industry in Norway in total decreased with 17 per cent from 1970 to 1990, the decline amounted to only 2 per cent in Møre and Romsdal.[16]

Knowledge dissemination and entrepreneurship, 1917–1953

The inter-war period represented a leap forward for business establishments in Norway. The number of enterprises grew by 37 per cent from 1930 to 1937. The pivotal role of 'know-how' disseminated through cooperative relations between actors has been underlined as the basis of this transformation.[17]

One important institution in this respect was the small business advisory branches, *Småindustrikontorer* (SIK). The first one was established in Kristiansund in the sub-region Nordmøre in the county of Møre and Romsdal, in 1926. The Kristiansund branch alone assisted in setting up 62 firms until 1932. It received and answered around 6,000 letters in 1931 from different parts of the country. In 1930, six branches of SIK were set up in Norway, while altogether 21 were established until 1935.[18]

The establishing of SIK branches was the result of joint efforts by business, professions and voluntary organisations, all aiming at creating new employment opportunities. The economic crises in the 1920s and 1930s furthered 'know-how' networking on the regional level. The assistance of the SIKs improved the ability of businesses to take advantage of decentralised production located close to raw material resources and cheap labour, and simultaneously to centralise marketing and sales functions, thus enhancing the possibility to monitor market trends and suggest utilisation of new technology and new products. These mechanisms in many cases laid the basis for developing high-technology small businesses within the furniture industry.

The STI was set up in 1916. To a larger extent than the SIKs, the purpose of the STI was to transfer knowledge from the national to the regional level. The cooperation between the STI and the SIKs promoted a gradual technological and financial development of firms.

The combination of low wages and investments in technology turned out to be a dynamic element in expanding the businesses. The SIKs were created on the initiative of local business firms, organisations and local authorities, while the government played an active part in setting up and financing the STI. The main characteristic of the STI's work in the 1930s seems to be the effective building up of *bi-lateral* relations between business and knowledge producers through course-works and advisory services.

In the post-war period, the STI came to be considered 'an important element in the industrial policy towards the SMEs'.[19] These ambitions materialised especially in the 1960s, first in the creation of a comprehensive *coursework* adapted to the SMEs needs, second in *contracts* with enterprises in implementing long-term planning, economic analyses, technological and organisational development, production process analyses and automation, materials handling and productivity, and third in engaging in *projects* and *R&D related activities* designed to facilitate application of know-how to the SMEs needs as well as the general conveyance of actual knowledge.[20]

Internationalisation and regionalisation of knowledge dissemination, 1953–1987

In order to depict the systemic character of this period, we need to briefly outline some formative processes prior to the establishing of the NPI in 1953, taking place within the framework of the STI.

The regional expansion of the STI

The STI expanded its activity after the war, like in the department dealing with the furniture and wood processing industry. In 1961, the STI set up a one-year part-time coursework for leaders in this industry. Apart from different kinds of courseworks, the direct business counsel activity was the most comprehensive, including for example advice in long-term planning.[21]

Another department organised business, labour and work management relations. Before the war, the department had organised courses in production organisation and labour management that attracted great interest and attendance. In 1948, courses in Training Within Industry for Supervisors (TWI), largely American and British influenced, became popular.[22] The need for this kind of know-how was in the ship-building industry in particular. Management courses at different levels were at the core of this training, which included topics like cooperative relations, work instructions, how to create and manage discussions on the shop-floor level, work methods, continuing cooperation process development and development of training programmes. The *rationalisation* office within the department created new courses in work organisation and production process management from the 1930s.[23] In 1948, this office was made an own department. The American-inspired Method-Time-Measurement (MTM) system was introduced in 1952, a technique combining frequence studies, factory planning, production planning and statistical quality control. The STI also set up a *business administration and economics* department in 1958, partly funded by the NPI. In 1963, this department promoted shorter courses in management for smaller businesses, and in 1965, a number of courses in business administration and economics, accounting, financing, investment prognoses, taxation regulations, profitability assessment, office organisation and marketing were introduced.

The *regional work* of the STI was increasingly formalised and *organisationally* structured through the 1950s and 1960s. The STI set up a number of regional branches, and in 1964, a national office was designed to monitor and manage them. Business advisory services and courseworks as well as conferences for SME managers were central activities.[24]

While the activity in 1950 comprised 100 courses for over 1,000 attendants, in 1967, 6,000 participants attended 400 courses altogether.[25] In carrying out its work, the STI employed a network of business and labour institutions, universities, technical schools and vocational schools, research institutions and branch organisations. Especially concerning the development of SMEs, its ambition was to construct a knowledge and information dissemination system.[26] In the early 1960s, the national authorities put great emphasis on expanding the business advisory services and urged the establishing of new regional branches.[27] According to the STI, several 'stages' had to be facilitated in the transfer of knowledge. First, the companies needed capacity to collect information on new research achievements. Second, they needed competence to decide on its applicability. The third stage was deciding on implementation. The STI stressed that a qualified dissemination *system* was required and was paramount to improve business innovativeness and competitiveness.[28] In Great Britain, according to the STI, it had been estimated that *system failures*, i.e. shortcomings in the dissemination of knowledge, equated 10 per cent out of the total investment in research and development, while in the USA, it had been estimated a loss of 200 million dollars in 1961 within the electro-technical industry only, due to such system failure. The STI subsequently concluded that the systematical dissemination of knowledge was a crucial factor in economic growth.[29]

Accordingly, a two-fold challenge had to be met. First, institutions that could present new results in a way that companies were able to understand were highly required. Second, companies needed tools that enabled them to evaluate the applicability of knowledge. A major challenge, therefore, was to establish a far better system, labelled an information and knowledge *'dissemination chain'*. In this chain, national documentation centres should connect vertically to branch institutes or regional and local information institutions. Horizontally, conferences should facilitate the dissemination of the expertise found within the institutions, because so much depended on transforming and infusing formal knowledge with the more informal, local and tacit expertise.[30]

In the beginning of the 1960s, several authorities indeed worked towards expanding business advisory services in the regions. A public report published in 1962 on the request of the Department of Industry advocated the need to use SME consultants in the regions. In responding to the report, the STI underlined the need to coordinate this activity with the STI, local technical schools, small business offices and branch organisations.[31]

In 1962, the STI sought to establish three new regional business counsellors in Ålesund, Stavanger in South-Western part of Norway and Skien in East Norway. One reason for expanding the work in these regions was that the STI 'in recent years has tried to meet an increasing demand for advisory services especially in these regions'. The form of expansion was not at all without importance, however. Local milieus should play an important part in expanding the *infrastructure* of business advisory services. Hence, it was stressed that the regional advisors needed to operate in collaboration with local technical know-how, and preferably conduct the work from an office located nearby or at a technical school. The STI advocated the principle that the location of advisory services should be based on *industrial districts* (*næringsdistrikter*), rather than according to formal county administrative boarders. In general, there was reason to believe that 'the local net of contacts must be emphasised in particular, and the regional work must be related to local traditions and industrial districts established over time'.[32] In this way, the system was based on existing regional learning networks.

In the 1960s, the STI had established workshops for managers of smaller businesses, *bedriftslederskoler*. These schools were directed towards specific industries, like the furniture industry and the automobile service sector.[33] Since 1963, moreover, a management workshop for craft and smaller businesses had been running as a pilot project. By 1967, it was included in the formal education system for vocational training under the Ministry of Church and Education, substituting the fourth year of the apprenticeship school. However, both the authorities and the STI realised a need for developing a more advanced management education for this sector as a part of STI's domain.[34] In general, there was a substantial demand drive for industry specific courses which the STI sought to meet. For example, courses in business administration were held all over the country in 1967 on the request of the engineering industry.[35]

Participation was a key word in the activities of the STI. The coursework often required the active role of the participants. Many courses were based on discussing actual cases or problems found in the participating firms. For instance, this method was important in the rationalisation effort, like courses in production techniques and work simplification and standardisation, including topics like product analyses, process analyses and method analyses. By the end of the coursework, it was required that each participating manager was able to 'implement' or 'translate' the knowledge by suggesting improvements of current practices within his business.[36] This method clearly required a great deal of trust between the participants and the STI. The STI in this way acted as a *proactive* element in the regional dissemination of know-how.[37]

The collaboration between STI and NPI

NPI, in collaboration with the STI, opened up channels for the transfer of international trends and know-how to the national innovation system, and through the regional branches, also to the regions. During the 1950s, for example, a number of American consultants visited the regions. At the national level the NPI in 1964 entered a cooperative agreement with The Foundation for Research on Human Behaviour, at Ann Arbor, Michigan. Academic institutions like this one seemed to have been important to the Norwegian productivity effort.[38] The NPI representatives also studied business practices in Germany, Switzerland, Holland and England. Also the European Productivity Agency (EPA) was an important connection to international knowledge producing institutions.[39]

Both horizontally and vertically the STI and the NPI jointly established channels for regional dissemination of knowledge. The NPI made substantial efforts to develop cooperation through networks between SMEs within subjects like accounting and marketing.[40] An important initiative was to establish local productivity offices in districts dominated by small firms. In 1959, one of the offices in Møre and Romsdal, for example, enjoyed the membership of 15 different organisations, representing almost all industries, craft-related industries and wholesale trade in the sub-region. All in all, our sources illustrate that the NPI was supported with enthusiasm by a variety of businesses and organisations.[41]

A cornerstone in the STI/NPI activity was a series of meetings involving the managers and middle managers of firms together with external consultants or lecturers and professors from the *Norges Handelshøyskole* (NHH, the Norwegian School for Economics and Business Administration in Bergen) called '*bedriftsledersamlinger*'. The implementation of the meetings was paralleled by a wide range of different kinds of management courses. These were normally overbooked by top managers eager to learn. They covered a range of subjects like accounting, general management and business administration (sale, marketing, market analysis). Also, through a 1–2 months long process, firms were investigated and improvements in functional as well as general management techniques were suggested. Since the work was conceived of as successful,[42] it encouraged the NPI to plan the setting up of local branches in Østfold, Sørlandet, Rogaland and Trøndelag. A substantial number of single company analysis was carried out until 1965. During 1966, the work was expanded by introducing a method of systematic 'learning from each other'. Managerial teams from different enterprises visited and studied each other's firms, and the visits were followed up by conferences that facilitated discussions between businesses.[43]

From the evidence presented, it can be concluded that an effective knowledge dissemination system had been established at regional level by the late 1960s. Vertically, the STI and the NPI connected their activities to a number of educational institutions at national and regional levels. Horizontally, the management conferences, the meetings, the firm diagnoses, the sub-contracting programmes, the networking between firms and the courseworks made it possible to spread information and new knowledge of innovations to regional firms. Both the NPI and the STI took care to adapt their approaches to management and management training and education to already established learning processes in the regional innovation systems. Thus, they facilitated the flow of information between actors. The system also promoted an active interaction between the national and the regional systems of innovation.

According to the concepts outlined in the above theoretical introduction, the growing activity within the productivity movement depended not only on the general ability to translate and transfer know-how to national and regional contexts, but also on the ability to establish viable transfer channels, mechanisms and processes, in other words *arenas* for the flow of knowledge. Essentially, the system promoted qualification for management of regional business, as it was based on business-to-business networking and interaction between knowledge providers and businesses.

It is not within the scope of this article to assess the effect of this qualification system at company level and establish a causal link between the dissemination system and business performance. Recent research has, however, depicted the essential role of the dissemination system at a *networking* level. The furniture industry in Møre and Romsdal experienced a serious crisis in the beginning of the 1980s, lagging behind its Swedish and Danish competitors, even in the domestic market. Due to networking between managers in the furniture industry, engaging experts at the STI, and the national and international contacts of the NPI, they were able to get insight into the technological modernisation of their competitors. Furthermore, the networking tradition played a paramount role, as none of the companies could single-handedly mobilise financial resources to implement the technology. Hence, a number of companies joined forces, and a modern production unit was set up in Sykkylven in the sub-region Sunnmøre, which could be utilised by the different companies.[44]

Inclusion of the RCs?

In 1969, the idea of setting up Regional University Colleges (RCs) with a two-year business administration education constituting the cornerstone of the curriculum was formally proposed. Two were established in Møre and Romsdal. During the 1970s, regional businesses expressed expectations that these colleges, primarily to meet a need for management education.[45]

During the 1970s, the NPI had put much effort into strengthening the link between regional business and the RCs.[46] A NPI project was created in 1968 to analyse problems related to forging the links between research and businesses in general. In Møre and Romsdal, the NPI influenced the setting up of a coursework at the Molde University College focusing on management development and long-term planning. Several comprehensive conferences on management education and training were held at the Molde University College in 1972, and local companies were quite well represented at these conferences.[47] Furthermore, a project on relations between SMEs and local governments was set up in cooperation with the Oppland College in 1979.[48]

In 1972, the NPI established a committee to develop a nation-wide system for management education for SMEs and promote ‘a comprehensive regional cooperation between RCs, technical colleges, the STI and NPI, local business organisations and local as well as county authorities’.[49] One obvious advantage was that a regional system would be better prepared to deal with region-specific problems in different regions. In the early 1980s, furthermore, two government appointed committees suggested to launch a policy for regional dissemination integrating the advisory institutions and the RCs.[50] A better coordinated system was thought to promote innovation, not the least in the SME.[51] Public support to coordinate the efforts of RCs and business advisory services was recommended.[52] No doubt, the strengthening of the relations in a regional dissemination system was seen as a crucial element in public SME policy and regional policy.[53] These perspectives were adopted by the central authorities through a number of parliamentary documents which emphasised the dissemination issue.[54]

The STI was intended to be a cornerstone in regional knowledge dissemination systems. The government in this respect focused on the need to increase the transfer of knowledge from research to industry.[55] The ability of the STI to establish a closer link to the RCs and regional technical colleges emerged as a precondition for a strengthened dissemination system.[56] The STI carried on its work and, in fact, also developed quite extensive contacts with some of the RCs and the technical colleges, however, mainly to shorter management courses and technological issues at the technical colleges. The contacts were frequent also to some industries, in particular the furniture, wood processing and mechanised industries. Some of the regional branches of the STI developed close collaboration with the state governed information services in the local municipalities, *Statlig industriell informasjonstjeneste* (INKO).[57] A broad national investigation of the role of 150 knowledge-providers concluded in 1986 that the STI/INKO and the *Norges Tekniske Høgskole* (NTH/SINTEF) were the ‘stars’ in the knowledge networking, whereas the research institutes at branch level and the RCs appeared to be isolated milieus.[58]

The RCs experienced an academic drift that did not allow for closer contact with the business sector and which placed the RCs primarily as an actor in the national innovation system. The RCs succeeded in their strive to become insiders in the university system. In this process, the national orientation totally overshadowed the initiatives towards regional business.[59] However, as the need to engage the RCs and also regional research institutions, set up in the early 1980s, was constantly reproduced in the regional and industrial policy, one hoped that setting up a new institution under the county authorities in 1987 should be a better instrument for forging this link.

The County-administered dissemination system, 1987–1998

The end of the 1970s witnessed a shift in industrial, economic and regional policy that effected the regional innovation system. The period up to 1980 has been labelled the *redistribution* policy. It aimed at economic and industrial growth in the less developed regions through re-allocation of resources from the central and more prosperous areas and sectors. It was a policy, it is claimed, of transferring resources *to* the regions. Its focus was mainly larger projects involving larger businesses and higher education. From around 1980, however, much more emphasis was placed on stimulating the local innovative capacity in the regions by mobilising the capabilities *inside* the regions. The role of knowledge dissemination and the interaction between SMEs and the RCs and R&D institutions was underlined. Establishing a regional infrastructure for *innovation* became a key issue and the SMEs the target for interventions through public intervention programmes.[60] While not disputing the fact that there was a change in industrial and regional policy in the early 1980s, the historical evidences of the dissemination systems in the period 1917–53, and 1953–87, demonstrate that the regional orientation was not at all new, in fact it was carried out *in practice* before the 1980s. The dissemination system in operation until 1987 was, however, incapable of engaging the RCs in the regional innovation system.

In 1987, the responsibility for the knowledge dissemination in the regions was handed over to county authorities, with the intention to improve the flow of knowledge between regional institutions, and to include the RCs in this flow. A new counselling institution, *Møre and Romsdal Bedriftsrådgivning* (MRB), was set up, and the STI was dissolved.

Despite these efforts, a considerable frustration because of lack of coordination within the dissemination system has emerged. And although a number of regional 'competence centres', regional research centres, science parks, technology centres and innovation centres have been set up since the early 1980s, few of them have become active partners in dissemination of knowledge on regional level.[61] As a matter of fact, the regional dissemination and innovation system has increasingly been conceived of as intransparent and programme-focused, and has not facilitated the inclusion of the RCs and regional research institutions into the dissemination system.[62]

Recently, complaints about the intransparency in the regional innovation system have been voiced.[63] The public intervention programmes set up to facilitate the transfer of knowledge to the SME sector have so far had rather limited success.[64] As previously mentioned, studies argue that, for example, Møre and Romsdal no longer stands out as an advanced regional innovation system. A comprehensive study of regional innovation structures in Western Norway concludes that two thirds of all companies want assistance in launching new products. About 60 per cent of the companies investigated want support for their national and international marketing efforts, and about the same percentage expressed need for financial support in this respect. Many firms also articulate a need for general management support, although less frequently than for technological and financial support. According to the report, 'The increasing need for general management support results from the fact that the markets in several industries have been globalised and become more demanding. Partly, the companies have difficulties in defining what particular support service they need to cope with these circumstances. Therefore, pro-active awareness raising services and high overall level of transparency in respect to the available services is necessary'.[65]

The vast majority, it is concluded, has no overview of available services. Only 2 per cent of all companies regard their understanding as good; 74 per cent say they have no clue or at best limited insight into which innovation support actor is providing what types of services. Yet, recent evidences from Møre and Romsdal show that over 50 per cent of the companies in the region have costs connected to innovation, especially in testing and launching new products. Such costs are in fact common also in smaller companies, and companies with less than 10 employees spend more than 25 per cent of their innovation costs on R&D-related services. However, firms cooperate more frequently with partners in other regions or nationally than with partners in their own region. There is a very limited interaction with higher education and research institutions in the region.[66]

Moreover, although there is reason to believe that the RCs play a more significant role for the middle management level in public sector and in the service sector, within the educational system so far no management education with a regional 'design' has been established. The fact that regional business managers generally do not graduate from regional colleges raises the question of what role these key institutions of the modern dissemination system play in enhancing localized learning and innovation.

Furthermore, surveys of different Norwegian regions have highlighted the fact that regional businesses increasingly recruit top managers with high formal education from national institutions, mainly graduates from technical universities and business schools. In the case of Møre and Romsdal, for instance, in 1995, 84 per cent of top

Table 2.1 Percentage of upper echelon managers with higher educational background in three regions

Region (county)	*Recruited before 1986*	*Recruited 1986–1995*
Møre and Romsdal	52	84
Akershus	77	98
Agder	33	69

Sources: O. Bjarnar and H. Gammelsæter, *Næringslivslederes utdanning og eierposisjon. En historisk undersøkelse fra Møre og Romsdal*, Research report 9501 (Møre Research Centre, Molde, 1995). For Akershus, see T. C. Dalby and H. Lian, *Næringslivslederes utdanning og eierposisjon i Akershus*, diplomoppgave (Norwegian School of Management (BI), 1996). For Agder, consult T. Kjempekjenn, M. Venemyr and M. L. Mæhlum, *Næringslivslederes utdanning og eierposisjon i Agder*, diplomoppgave (Norwegian School of Management (BI), 1996).

managers recruited between 1986 and 1995 had a higher education, compared to 52 per cent of managers recruited before 1986. Among the managers recruited from 1986 to 1995 with a higher education, only 8 per cent had graduated from university colleges in the region compared to 9 within the group recruited before 1986. The same pattern goes for Akershus and Agder (see Table 1).[67]

Summary and concluding remarks

In this paper, we have described the historical development of knowledge dissemination systems in regional Norway. Our point of departure was ideas advocated by recent innovation theorists, particularly the idea that such systems should nurture localised and interactive learning processes rather than impose top-down innovation strategies that are more or less disconnected from the local innovation processes. We have argued that an important implication of this view is that management knowledge is given a substantial local flavour, although the ability to integrate novel externally derived knowledge is important in order to prevent lock-in situations in local learning. The requirement for the construction of regional knowledge dissemination and management qualification systems is therefore their ability to establish knowledge flows in which local and international knowledge is integrated, made sense of and connected to local interactive learning processes.

Our historical account of the development of the subsystems that promoted management education and knowledge dissemination in Norway, resulted in the identification of three historical periods or phases between 1917 and our decade. Each of these periods was characterised if not entirely by different approaches, so at least by different emphasis on diverse approaches to the creation of knowledge flows. In the first period from 1917 until 1953, institutions like the STI and the SIKs provided an extensive flow of knowledge to business entrepreneurs. This flow of knowledge had major impact on the industrial development, especially in the 1930s, but also after 1945. In the second period, following the setting up of the NPI in 1953, the collaboration between the STI and the NPI gradually developed into agencies that rather effectively sensed and through the use of different methods – consulting, conferences, business meetings and courseworks – answered many of the different demands of regional business. A particular characteristic of the system in this period was the ability to create arenas where practitioners and knowledge providers met to discuss and sometimes solve business problems. The period, however, also witnessed the introduction of a regional system of formal management education and efforts to integrate formal education into the previous system that primarily promoted knowledge flows through more loose or informal dissemination mechanisms. As it turned out, the efforts to have the regional university colleges develop and run courses directed towards specific industrial or vocational needs largely failed. A necessary, but not sufficient, explanation for this was the academisation process within the colleges. The combination of assisting local business while at the same time meet academic requirements turned out to be difficult. Another explanation is that the expectations towards the RCs within the regional and industrial policy in this respect were not founded on concrete institutional analysis, and that a 'mechanised' approach, merely saying that the flow of knowledge could be facilitated through better coordination between partners, was reproduced almost unchanged. The momentum of the wave of regional college establishments had the effect, however, of shifting the balance between knowledge dissemination and formal management education.

The third and subsequent period was introduced in 1987, as the county authorities was given the responsibility of public dissemination of knowledge within the region. Based on a number of public and semi-public reports, as well as recent research, we conclude that the period was characterised by the primary emphasis on formal education and, in knowledge dissemination terms, the rather weak position and connection between other public service providers. Whereas the relations between managers and service providers in the first two periods stimulated many joint activities, the most recent period is generally characterised by little communication between the allegedly key knowledge actors in the innovation systems, the regional university colleges and regional managers. Although much emphasis has been put on innovation issues in the 1980s and 1990s, and innovation having been expected to be promoted through regional infrastructures, the arenas of communication that were created in previous times are now few and restricted. This seems paradoxical against the changes in business managers' backgrounds. Despite the fact that much larger proportions of managers now than before have higher educational backgrounds, the relations to the regional academic institutions are generally weak. This can be explained by the fact that few of the recruits to executive managerial positions seem to have graduated from the regional colleges. This poses the question of the extent to which the system of regional management education has been able to nurture processes of localised learning and innovation.

Notes

1 Asheim, B. T. and A. Isaksen, 'Location, Agglomeration and Innovation: Towards regional Innovation Systems in Norway?', *European Planning Studies*, Vol. 5, No. 3 (1995), p. 301.
2 B.-Å. Lundvall (ed.), *National Systems of Innovation: Towards a theory of Innovation and Interactive Learning* (London and New York, 1992). Consult also M. Porter, *The Competitive Advantage of Nations* (Macmillan, 1990), p. 19.
3 Asheim and Isaksen, 'Location, Agglomeration and Innovation', p. 300.
4 Ibid.
5 Lundvall, *National Systems of Innovation*, p. 12.
6 The character of globalisation, the alleged turn from Fordist modes of production and regulation to flexible specialisation, the factual extent of regional innovation systems, the character, strength and weaknesses of networks related to dynamic processes or lock-in and path-dependency, respectively, the required mode of public intervention to promote or sustain such systems, as well as a number of related themes, have all been subjected to a lot of debate. For a few examples, see Asheim and Isaksen, 'Location, Agglomeration and Innovation', pp. 299–330; B. T. Asheim, 'Industrial Districts as 'Learning Regions': a Condition for Prosperity', *European Planning Studies*, Vol. 4, No. 4 (1996), pp. 377–400; B. T. Asheim, 'Flexible specialisation, industrial districts and small firms: a critical appraisal', in H. Erneste and V. Meier (eds), *Regional Development and Contemporary Industrial Response: Extending Flexible Specialisation* (London, 1992), pp. 45–46; see also in this book B. Jessop, 'Post Fordism and flexible specialisation: incommensurable, contradictory, or just plain different perspectives?' and A. J. Scott and M. Storper, 'Regional development reconsidered', consult furthermore M. J. Piore and C. F. Sabel, *The Second Industrial Divide. Possibilities for Prosperity* (New York, 1984), P. Hirst and J. Zeitlin, 'Flexible specialisation versus post-Fordism: theory, evidence and policy implications', *Economy and Society*, Vol. 20, No. 1 (February 1991); A. Amin and N. Thrift (eds), *Globalization, Institutions, and Regional Development in Europe* (Oxford, 1994).

7 See H. Wiig, 'Innovativ aktivitet og innovasjonssystemer i Møre og Romsdal og Finnmark', in A. Isaksen (ed.), *Innovasjoner, næringsutvikling og regionalpolitikk* (Kristiansand, 1997), p. 149.

8 Lundvall (ed.), *National Systems of Innovation,* and A. Isaksen (ed.), *Innovasjoner*, respectively.

9 This distinction is made in different articles in Isaksen (ed.), *Innovasjoner,* see for example B. T. Asheim and A. Isaksen, 'Regionale innovasjonssystemer – en teoretisk diskusjon', p. 70.

10 The managers' positions in dissemination of knowledge is discussed in R. G. Havelock *et al.*, *Planning for Innovation: A Comparative Study of the Literature on the Dissemination and Utilization of Scientific Knowledge* (Ann Arbor, University of Michigan, 1969); E. M. Rogers, *Diffusion of Innovations* (New York, 1995). For a recent overview, see O. Bjarnar and M. Kipping, 'The Marshall Plan and the transfer of US management models to Europe: an introductory framework', in M. Kipping and O. Bjarnar (eds), *The Americanisation of European Business. The Marshall Plan and the transfer of US management models* (London and New York, 1998), pp. 1–18.

11 See especially P. Stevrin and Å. Uhlin, *Tillit, kultur och regional utvecklingaspekter på Blekinge som mentalt kulturlandskap* (Blekinge, 1996).

12 Asheim and Isaksen, 'Regionale innovasjonssystemer', p. 58.

13 See A. Isaksen, 'Kunnskapsaktører i teoreien om regionale innovasjonssystemer', in H. Gammelsæter (ed.), *Innovasjonspolitikk, kunnskapsflyt og regional utvikling* (Norges forskningsråd, 2000).

14 R. P. Amdam and O. Bjarnar, 'Regional Business Networks and the Diffusion of American Management and Organisational Models to Norway, 1945–65', in *Business History*, Vol. 39, No. 1 (January 1997) and same authors; 'The regional dissemination of American productivity models in Norway in the 1950s and 1960s', in Kipping and Bjarnar (eds); *Americanisation*, pp. 91–113.

15 For the historical perspective, see, for example, O. Wicken, *Entreprenørskap i Møre og Romsdal: Et historisk perspektiv*, Step group report 21 (Oslo, 1994), same author, *Norsk fiskeriteknologipolitiske mål i møte med regionale kulturer*, Step group report 17 (Oslo, 1994). Consult also A. Løset, *Likskap og lagdeling. Fylkeshistorie for Møre og Romsdal 1920–1972* (Oslo, 1996). For examples of a present more sceptical approach to Møre and Romsdal, see Asheim and Isaksen, 'Location, Agglomeration and Innovation', H. Wiig and M. Wood, *What comprises a regional innovation system?*, Step group report (Oslo, 1995), and O. Spilling, 'Industrial reconstruction and the re-emergence of small scale production', in *Industriutvikling og sysselsetting i et regionalt perspektiv. Seminarrapport* (Arbeidsliv-Historie-Samfunn, serie B (Bergen 1993). Consult furthermore H. Wiig, 'Innovativ aktivitet'; and P. Heydebreck and E. Arnold, *Regional Innovation Structures in Western Norway*, RITTS report 111 (Regional Innovation and Technlogy Transfer Strategies and Infrastructures), edited by B. Fjellstad (1997).

16 Andersen, H. W., 'Norsk skipsbyggingsindustri gjennom 100 år', in E. Lange (ed.) *Teknologi i virksomhet: Verkstedsindustri i Norge etter 1840* (Oslo, 1989); Hanisch, T. J and E. Lange, *Veien til velstand* (Oslo, 1986); *Historisk statistikk 1978*, table 43; Isaksen, A. and O. Spilling, *Regional*

utvikling og små bedrifter (Kristiansand, 1996), see tables 5.1 and 5.2; Kamsvåg, J. L., *Med nål og tråd gjennom 100 år: Bekledningsarbeiderforbundet 1890–1990* (Oslo, 1990).

17 See E. Lange, 'Småbedrifter og moderne teknologi', in F. Sejersted (ed.), *Vekst gjennom krise* (Oslo, 1982). The reconstruction of the inter-war period is mainly built on Lange.

18 Sources from five of the branches document that at least 15,000 advices were given to businesses in 1931. In 1934, they assisted in setting up hundreds of firms employing 4,000 new workers this year only.

19 NOU 1984: 19 *STI – Statens teknologiske institutt*, p. 13.

20 Ibid. As late as in the 1980s approximately 70%–75% of the STIs regional activity, channelled through regional branches (distriktskontorer), was devoted to economic advisory services, organisational development, planning and marketing. 75% of all its activity involved firms with less than 100 employees.

21 The STI, for example, facilitated an extensive cooperation between the furniture business federation, *Møbelprodusentenes Landsforening*, and the corresponding designers' federation, *Interiørarkitektenes Landsforbund*. Besides long-term planning, companies wanted assistance on a number of subjects. Producers from Møre and Romsdal were active in this respect, and especially a great number of producers from Sunnmøre feature in the sources. For a few examples, see National Archives, Statens Teknologiske Institutt (hereafter NA/STI), Boxes 145 (1962) and 170 (1970). This pattern is, accordingly, an example of the dynamics within regional innovation systems themselves.

22 Confer *Statens teknologiske instiutt* (Oslo, 1967), p. 48.

23 In 1947, the department employed its own rationalisation expert, who introduced new courses and consultations in work-time-measurement studies. The political setting is interesting, as one reason for his appointment was an agreement between the national federation of industries, *Norges Industriforbund* and the national labour organisation, *Landsorganisasjonen*, saying that the shop floor stewards, *tillitsmennene*, should gain insight into the production and productivity processes through a politically *neutral* institution. This was a kind of 'neutral' position and role definition the STI consistently throughout the post-war era strived to maintain, see *Statens teknologiske institutt* (1967), p. 51.

24 Although after the Second World War, the Norwegian government connected the strategy for construction of the welfare state essentially to industrial expansion. At the core of this expansion was promoting the heavy export industries. It is claimed, therefore, that the traditional industries like furniture and textile were given less priority. In this sector, the governmental policy mainly aimed at rationalising businesses and thereby promoting the setting up of larger units to achieve improved performance in scale and scope. See, for example, R. P. Amdam, S. Knutsen and L. Thue; *Bedrift og samfun* (Bergen-Sandviken, 1997), p. 60, T. J. Hanisch and E. Lange, *Veien til velstand* (Oslo, 1986). But the central authorities also emphasised the development of counselling services for SMEs in the districts, confer *Stm. nr. 6 (1959–60) Om utbygging av industrien i distriktene*.

25 *Statens teknologiske institutt* (1967), p. 79.

26 Initially, this process was coupled to the growing focus on regional development in Norwegian politics. In 1955, the board of the fund for development of Northern Norway, *Nord-Norgefondet*, encouraged the STI to set up a local branch in Narvik in order to facilitate courses, act as a consultancy and assist the regional planning authorities, *Områdeplanleggingskontorene*. This setting-up resulted in a fast increasing course activity in the area. In 1959, a regional branch emerged in Trøndelag, helped forward by financial input from the regional development programme *Trøndelagsplanen*. See *Statens teknologiske institutt* (1967).
27 *Stm. nr. 6 (1959–60) Om utbygging av industrien i distriktene.*
28 *Statens teknologiske institutt* (1967) p. 83.
29 Ibid., p. 86.
30 Ibid., pp. 85–90.
31 Referred to in STI documents were the Siem committee and the Danielsen committee, respectively. The Danielsen committee was named after its chair, Rationalisation Director Reidar Danielsen, and was set up in 1959.
32 See NA/STI, Box 142, letter to the actual Ministry December 21 1962, and box 143, letter to the Ministry 8 February 1962 from Hans Hauge at the STI.
33 Cf. NA/STI, Box 182, Annual Report 1968, preliminary version.
34 Ibid.
35 See NA/STI, Box 182, Annual Report 1967, preliminary version.
36 As described in NA/STI, Box 173, letter from the STI, engineer Cornelius Gundersen, to A/S Myrens Mekaniske Verksted, Oslo, January 6 1969.
37 NA/STI, Box 174, letter from Hans Hauge, STI to *Møre og Romsdal Fylkesorganisasjon for Håndverk og Industri*, 22 October 1963.
38 One of the most busy was Walter H. Channing, who held a number of courses in rationalisation and sales psychology in 1958 in Møre & Romsdal and even acted as a consultant for some of the trading firms. Channing was executive director of the American association of retailers. In 1955, five American experts visited 15 different businesses in the region. It is known that Channing promoted the so-called 'self-selection' principle, and reconstructing the shops according to this. His visit furthermore led to a lot of local plans of modernisation of buildings and sales techniques.
39 In 1959, for example, Franklin G. Moore, professor of industrial management, and professor of human relations Norman F. Maier, both coming from this university, toured Norway disseminating their research. Some experts from the University of Michigan were also connected to the European Productivity Agency or EPA, like Dr Arnold S. Tannenbaum, a specialist in work psychology and industrial sociology. Moreover, the EPA financed a tour to Oslo and Bergen in 1959 for professor in financial research, Wilford John Eiteman, also from Michigan. The NPI established contacts, furthermore, to the British Institute of Management, which each year held conferences for upper echelon managers. The NPI closely monitored conferences held in different European countries. Other American experts missioning Norway in 1959–61 were, for a few examples, R. W. Shepard, University of California, R. K. Yaumnitz, University of Minnesota, Dr. Harry. A. Johnson, Virginia State College. For more details, see NA/NPI, Box 649, diverse issues of NPI-nytt.

40 The *network* concept is applied in a broad sense in this paper. The concept of *channel* is likewise complex and connected to the diffusion of innovations. Channels are connecting actors and institutions in a way that messages are communicated between them. See, for example, Rogers, *Diffusion of Innovations*. For application of these concepts in a regional context, consult Amdam and Bjarnar, 'The Regional Dissemination'.
41 For details, see Amdam and Bjarnar, 'Regional Business Networks'.
42 NA/NPI, Box 649, NPI-nytt 25 April 1958.
43 For details consult Amdam and Bjarnar, 'The regional dissemination'. In 1962, the NPI realised a need to work more systematically according to a long-term plan, especially concerning the actual needs of businesses. Among eleven priorities were increasing efforts to promote implementation of long-term planning in companies, develop programmes for management education and training, improve education and training in marketing, create a more advanced system for business administration education, stimulate and support the local productivity branches, stimulate research within industrial psychology and industrial sociology and improve dissemination of new information. It was hardly a coincidence that long-term planning was given high priority. This was seen as a crucial element in improving the performance of businesses.
44 See Bjarnar, O., 'Et regionperspektiv på innovasjonspolitikken', in H. Gammelsæter (ed.), *Innovasjonspolitikk*.
45 It is interesting to notice, that Andreas Bachmann, who later became dean of the college in Molde and the county's chief educational officer, was placed as a central actor in creating the curriculum of the study in business administration, had his previous carrier in the NPI in the Trøndelag region. In 1971, furthermore, the first lecturer in business administration in Molde was appointed as secretary of the NPI branch in Romsdal.
46 NA/NPI, Box 505 – project 979, Samspill distriktshøgskole – lokalsamfunn (Interaction between university colleges and local municipalities).
47 Confer NA/NPI, Box 267, diverse annual reports.
48 NA/NPI, Box 529 – project 1091.
49 NA/NPI Box 479, Management Education. The vision that the RCs should develop into instruments for regional development was also expressed by professor Svein M. Kile at the NHH, who in 1972 initiated a programme for organisational and managerial development in SMEs in the regions. Kile argued that no adequate *public policy* for transfer and dissemination of knowledge to the SMEs, despite the establishment of the RCs, had been developed on a national basis. He was, in particular, disappointed with the lack of initiative from the RCs, and their lack of ability to interact with businesses and their organisations in the regions. He launched the idea of a national plan for organisational development in the SME sector. In this plan, the RCs occupied a central position. The colleges should be systematically supported by and connected to a central milieu, comprising among others the STI, the NPI and the Norges Handelshøgskole (NHH). It was, however, essential to expand the work of the colleges and extended network by creating a system of cooperation between the SMEs themselves.
50 NOU 1981: 30 A *Forskning, teknisk utvikling og industriell innovasjon* and NOU 1984: 19 *STI – Statens teknologiske institutt*.

51 Confer NOU 1981: 30 A p. 10.
52 Ibid., p. 11.
53 Ibid., p. 14–15.
54 See *St. meld. nr 22* (1977–78) *Små og mellomstore industribedrifter, St. meld. nr. 54 (1980–81) Industripolitiske retningslinjer for de nærmeste år fremover, St. meld. nr. 54 (1982–83) Om teknisk-industriell forskning og utvikling.* Confer also NOU 1981: 4 *Utdanning for oljevirksomhet.*
55 *St. meld. nr. 54 (1980–81) Industripolitiske retningslinjer.*
56 NOU 1981: 30 A.
57 Confer NOU 1984: 19, tables 4.7, 4.8 and 4.9, pp. 21–23.
58 Johnstad, T., 'En rik flora av aktører for industriell nyskaping', in *Norges Industri* nr. 19 (1987).
59 Consult O. Bjarnar; *Academic Drift and the Market. Some Historical – Institutional Perspectives on the Growth of Private Higher Education in the region of Møre and Romsdal 1970–1986* (Molde, 1995).
60 See especially Arbo, P., 'Fra industriorientert til kunnskapsorientert modernisering. Om NordNorges plass i det moderne kunnskapssamfunnett', in E. O. Eriksen (ed.), *Det nye Nord-Norge. Avhengighet og modernisering i nord* (Bergen, 1996). Confer also A. Isaksen; 'Innovasjoner og politikk- en introduksjon', in Isaksen (ed.), *Innovasjoner*, pp. 20–21.
61 For an overview, see T. Johnstad, 'Kompetanse- og innovasjonssentre i Norge', *Plan & Arbeid* 1 (1986), pp. 3 –8. In fact, the only true success story was the collaboration between a number of different institutions in Narvik in Northern Norway.
62 See Heydebreck, Arnold and Fjellheim, *Regional Innovation Structures.* Structural factors may also have influenced the system, for a general overview see A. Skonhoft; 'Industrialisering og deindustrialisering in Norge 1960–1990', in A. Isaksen (ed.), *Innovasjoner*, pp. 112–127. The deindustrialisation of the regions during the 1980s could turn out to be an explanatory factor for the transition of the dissemination system. While the regions witnessed industrial expansion until the mid-1970s, the 1980s stands out as a period of decline in all Norwegian regions. Recent research has claimed that this pattern is common in most OECD countries. Hence, it seems to be the result of in-depth structural factors and not necessarily of specific national or regional characteristics or economic policy.
63 See, for example, Nærings-og energidepartementet; *Utfordringen-forskning og innovasjon for ny vekst*, (1996) (Aakvaagutvalget), Nærings- og energidepartementet; *Småbedriftsutvalget* (Hervikutvalget) (1996), and NOU 1996: 23 *Konkurranse, kompetanse og miljø. Næringspolitiske hovedstrategier* (Henriksenutvalget) (1996).
64 For an overview, see H. Gammelsæter and O. Bjarnar, *Kunnskapsflyt mellom akademia og regionalt næringsliv-fra retorikk til realitet*, Notat 1 (Molde, 1997).
65 Heydebreck, Arnold and Fjellheim, *Regional Innovation Structures*, p. 20.
66 Wiig, 'Innovativ aktivitet og innovasjonssystemer i Møre og Romsdal og Finnmark'.
67 In Agder, the number of managers with a higher education increased from 33 per cent among managers recruited before 1986 to 69 per cent among manager recruited from 1986 to 1995. Among these, 6 per cent had graduated from colleges in Agder in the first group compared to 7 per cent in the last group.

Postscript

Ove Bjarnar, Rolv Petter Amdam and Hallgier Gammelsæter

This article set out to explore the impact of management education on regional development. Drawing on our research on regional changes (Amdam & Bjarnar, 1997), regional culture (Bjarnar, Løseth, & Gammelsæter, 2004) and management education (Amdam, 1996), we chose to apply literature on regional innovation system as a theoretical framework. This concept was on the rise at the time, and we found it relevant for two reasons. First, it offered a dynamic approach to economic geography, which we saw as an invitation to historical studies. Second, it lent itself to analyse institutional and cultural explanations to regional development, as a supplement or alternative to economic and political factors.

This article addressed topics that still develop within the business history and regional studies literatures, such as the use of economic geography theories in business history (Amdam, Bjarnar, & Berge, 2020) and cultural explanations to regional development (Amdam, Lunnan, Bjarnar, & Halse, 2020). Regarding qualification for management positions, this article explores the role of formal higher education as well as training and competence-enhancing activities that exist outside the formal educational system. However, while trying to systematise the role of formal higher education (see Table 1 in this article), a similar exercise was unfortunately not done to categorise and systematise the role of other routes to management positions. The role of these 'other ways' to management positions than through formal higher education is still an unexplored research topic (Kipping, Amdam, & McGlade, 2020).

In retrospect, and in light of our own research post the *JIH* article, we can see that in the phases covered by our article formal and informal institutions were established over time that strengthened the intra-regional flow of knowledge while at the same time being embedded in global knowledge networks that were largely Americanised. The systematic building of regional knowledge networks promoted knowledge sharing among local actors and organisations, and flow of knowledge was institutionalised by commitment to this regional framework (i.e. Scott, 2008, for institutionalisation mechanisms).

Besides building on diverse formal qualifications, management qualification and recruitment were processed within this regional frame. Our article relates to several other publications based on empirical data from the same region. Already in the 1960s and 1970s, studies show that regional knowledge sharing also underpinned the formation of the successful maritime cluster in the region (Halse, 2014; Halse & Bjarnar, 2014a; Amdam & Bjarnar, 2015). Halse (2014) has argued that cluster cultures are strong, however challenged, and recently, Amdam et al. (2020) have demonstrated that the regional identity encourages the internationalisation of firms. Likewise, Nujen (2018) has shown how localised and intra-regional flows of knowledge propel business development and trigger regional businesses to backshore activities from abroad. We hypothesise that even today management and organisational practices are attached to regions. However, there is a scarcity of research about how regional systems have developed since the 1990s.

We admit that in the face of globalisation the picture of regional coherence has become increasingly blurred. In our article in *JIH*, we showed how devolvement of the regional dissemination system to the county level led to regional fragmentation of knowledge flows, and Bjarnar (2000) and Gammelsæter and Bjarnar (2000) further explored this development by addressing how knowledge flows were increasingly structured through the proliferation of short-lived public development programmes with the effect of disintegrating the historically developed dissemination system.

Since the late 1990s, in particular, internationalisation changed. While before, regional businesses tried to expand through setting up enterprises abroad, all of a sudden, multinational corporations acquired local firms incorporating them into their international networks (Amdam & Bjarnar, 2015). Bjarnar (2010), based on a number of in-depth interviews with regional leaders, indicated that globalisation promoted regional learning, but at the same time also knowledge flows through parallel expert networks less attached to the region. Halse and Bjarnar (2014a) underscored this picture arguing that this phenomenon could be related to tensions between historical modes of customised production and modes of standardised production for global mass markets. The challenge has been to implement both modes at the same time since they have implied a more delicate balance between a territorially confined value chain and globally dispersed production (Halse, 2014; Halse & Bjarnar, 2014a,b). The recent period of recession due to demand cutbacks within the oil and gas supply industries has triggered some focal businesses to enter new markets, for example, shifting focus from building oil service ships to produce cruise ships. Such strategies may require know-how residing more than before in networks external to the region. An interesting topic for further research would be, consequently, to what extent business partnerships and supplier networks get less attached than before to regional knowledge sharing.

Our *JIH* article (2001) together with Amdam and Bjarnar's (1997) and Gammelsæter and Bjarnar's (2000) study were important platforms for later work on management qualification, regional knowledge flows and the challenges posed by globalisation. Actually, seen through contemporary lenses, the *JIH* study should have been reprised and extended to our time. That would have revealed a more coherent picture of the state of regional systems in the era of globalisation. In this respect, researching the change and role of formal and informal institutions and not the least institutionalisation of regional and regional-global managerial practices would have provided another novel contribution to the regional innovation systems literature.

References

Amdam, R. P. (Ed.). 1996. *Management education and competitiveness: Europe, Japan, and the United States*. London: Routledge.

Amdam, R. P., & Bjarnar, O. 1997. Regional business networks and the diffusion of American management and organisational models to Norway, 1945–65. *Business History*, 39(1): 79–90.

Amdam, R. P., & Bjarnar, O. 2015. Globalization and the development of industrial clusters: Comparing two Norwegian clusters, 1900-2010. *Business History Review*, 89(4): 693–716.

Amdam, R. P., Bjarnar, O., & Berge, D. M. 2020. Resilience and related variety: The role of family firms in an ocean-related Norwegian region. *Business History*: 1–21.

Amdam, R. P., Lunnan, R., Bjarnar, O., & Halse, L. L. 2020. Keeping up with the neighbors: The role of cluster identity in internationalization. *Journal of World Business*, 55(5): 101125.

Bjarnar, O. 2000. Et regionsperspektiv på innovasjonspolitikken. In Hallgeir Gammelsæter (red.), *Innovasjonspolitikk, kunnskapsflyt og regional utvikling*. Trondheim: Tapir: 123–143.

Bjarnar, O. 2010. *Transformation of knowledge flow in globalizing industrial clusters*. Working paper, Molde University College, Molde.

Bjarnar, O., Løseth, A., & Gammelsæter, H. 2004. Næringskulturer på Nord-Vestlandet. In H. Gammelsæter, O. Bukve, & A. Løseth (Eds.), *Nord-Vestlandet - liv laga?*. Ålesund: Sunnmørsposten: 74–89.

Gammelsæter, H., & Bjarnar, O. 2000. Mellom akademia og regionalt næringsliv: betingelser for en vellykket innovasjonspolitikk. In Hallgeir Gammelsæter (red.), *Innovasjonspolitikk, kunnskapsflyt og regional utvikling*. Trondheim: Tapir: 45–59.

Halse, Lise L. 2014. Walking the path of change: Globalization of the maritime cluster in North West Norway. PhD thesis in Logistics 2014: 3, Molde University College, Molde.

Halse, Lise L., & Bjarnar, O. 2014a. The evolution of the maritime cluster in North West Norway, in Halse, Lise L. Walking the path of change: Globalization of the maritime cluster in North West Norway. PhD thesis in Logistics 2014: 3, Molde University College, Molde.

Halse, Lise L., & Bjarnar, O. 2014b. Social fields of knowledge flows: A regional cluster in a global context. In R. Rutten, P. Benneworth, D. Irawati, & F. Boekema (Eds.), *The social dynamics of innovation networks.* London: Routledge: 103–120.

Kipping, M., Amdam, R. P., & McGlade, J. 2020. Making managers: A fresh look. *Management & Organizational History*, 15(2): 91–105.

Nujen, Bella B. 2018. *The global shift-back: Backshoring from a knowledge perspective.* PhD thesis in Logistics 2018: 4, Molde University College, Molde.

Scott, W. R. 2008. *Institutions and organizations: Ideas and interests.* Thousand Oaks, CA: Sage Publications.

‘Neither a sleepy village nor a coarse factory town’

Skill in the Greater Springfield Massachusetts Industrial Economy, 1800–1990

Robert Forrant

Introduction

In the early 1800s, the Springfield Armory located in Western Massachusetts was the hub of an industrial district that stretched along the Connecticut River Valley between Hartford, Connecticut and White River Junction, Vermont, populated by networked groups of small metalworking and machine-making firms and a diverse group of final goods producers. The metalworking firms perfected numerous production techniques as they built tools, fixtures, molds, rifles, carriages, rail cars, and automobiles that were diffused to other regional producers. Thus, in the late 19th century and early 20th century, Springfield’s economic prosperity was built on a diversified manufacturing base deeply rooted in a set of industries that required at their core large numbers of highly skilled metalworkers and machinists. However, beginning in the 1960s, Springfield’s and the region’s industrial base, along with the thousands of skilled workers that had for generations been the foundation of a vibrant metalworking economy, suffered numerous plant closings that culminated with the dramatic shutdown in 1986 of the American Bosch plant.

Shouts of ‘Make them stay or make them pay’ reverberated off the walls of the International Union of Electrical Workers Local 206 meeting hall on February 6, 1986, for just hours earlier unionists learned that United Technologies Corporation, owner of the 76-year-old Bosch plant would shut the factory by July 1996. There had been a steady run of layoffs since UT acquired the factory in 1978; the production workforce had been slashed from 1,130 in 1979 to approximately 800, and numerous production lines and machine tools had been shifted to UT facilities in the South and abroad. The plant had been the only place

DOI: 10.4324/9780429059001

many of the unionists had ever worked. Donald Staples spent 36 years in the sprawling factory. An activist, he was able to send two sons to college on the steady wages he received. Staples had intended to work in the plant one summer before returning home to New Hampshire to attend college on the G.I. bill. Reflecting back he noted, 'It's sad. I didn't realize how much it meant to me, till I think about not going back in there. I can close my eyes and walk through the building. It's as if they tell you your mother's sick, but you never believe she is going to die'. A skilled machinist, Staples said he once would have been proud if his two sons had followed him into the Bosch; now he is happy they did not.

The Bosch closing was one in a series of shutdowns that rocked the Western Massachusetts economy. In 1968, the historic Springfield Armory ceased operations, costing the economy 2,000 skilled jobs. The Armory played a pivotal role in the growth of Springfield, and helped the city earn its late-19th century nickname of the 'industrial beehive'. The Armory closing was a harbinger of what was to follow, as one after another, ten precision metalworking firms with deep roots in the region were shuttered. While a detailed history of industry in the Connecticut River Valley is beyond the scope of this paper, in what follows I make a contribution to that endeavor through an examination of industrial growth in Springfield in the 19th century, late-20th century decline, and the current rebirth of metalworking, built on the activism of a vibrant industry trade association and a return to the skill base that once made the area a prominent global machinery and metalworking center.

There is a growing body of historical and contemporary evidence that the capacity of a particular industry or a regional or national economy to provide well-paying jobs and a broadly shared sustainable prosperity is contingent on an ability to learn new things and resolve production-related problems as they manifest themselves. Historical studies of the textile industry, machine tools, metalworking, plastics, and the semiconductor industry, specialty production, and heavy machinery demonstrate that when a systematic learning process among enterprises and institutions is nurtured knowledge is accumulated and the economic base strengthened. This paper, with its focus on individual firms and an industrial region, and the prominent role that skill played in the development of a vibrant metalworking district, helps to advance the field of industrial history and our understanding of the role that working people play in shaping that history. In what follows, I heed Philip Scranton's words in the inaugural issue of this journal and study an old 'regional and local territorial complex' to learn how and why it thrived and, equally important, why it came apart.[1]

Early History of Springfield Industry

Springfield began to secure its diverse manufacturing base soon after it was selected by Congress in 1776 to be a federal armory site.[2] The Armory became the hub of a flourishing industrial district along the Connecticut River populated by small metalworking and machine-making firms. Through most of the 19th century, Springfield and its environs enjoyed a comparative technological advantage over many other regions of the country due to the diffusion of Armory manufacturing techniques such as the utilization of gauges, fixtures, jigs and dies, and the availability of large numbers of skilled metalworkers who resided in the city. According to historian David Hounshell, 'The Armory acted both as a clearing house for technical information and a training ground for mechanics who later worked for private arms makers or for manufacturers of other goods'.[3]

The importance of collaboration for the diffusion of skill and technology was noted by Deyrup in her study of the region's gun making industry. She found that there was a rich contracting system among firms that promoted a 'spirit of cooperation and mutual aid' which had much to do 'with the rapid development of the industry in the first thirty years of the nineteenth century'. Much knowledge was exchanged between the Armory and contractors regarding interchangeability, manufacturing processes and machine tools.[4] By 1840, an industrial district spread along the Connecticut River Valley with small metalworking and machine making firms. Springfield alone housed 73 machine shops, six cotton factories, three paper mills, four printing concerns, two tool factories, a saw factory, and several saw and grist mills. By 1845, added to the industrial base were two brass foundries, two plow manufactories, and eight firms involved in the production of railroad cars and coaches. Rail connections to Boston and Worcester, Massachusetts, Hartford, Connecticut and Albany, New York sparked further growth in the 1850s. As a result of manufacturing growth, the population soared to 18,000 in 1850 from 1,500 in 1790.[5]

With industry growth there came an increase in the pool of skilled labor. The engineers and skilled craftsmen first employed at the Armory designed machine tools and developed a variety of innovative production techniques to manufacture rifles with interchangeable parts. Numerous skilled mechanics and machine designers took a stint at the Armory or another area shop in the early 19th century before travelling to other New England clusters of metalworking companies in Providence, Rhode Island, Worcester, Massachusetts, Hartford,

Connecticut and Windsor, Vermont. In this way, skills and knowledge were exchanged and the entire New England region grew in metalworking expertise.[6]

To support the growth of apprenticeship in metalworking and general respect for the trade, a mechanics' association was established in Springfield in 1824. The group supported a technical library and held quarterly meetings that featured addresses by members on such topics as 'Chemistry Connected with the Metals', 'The Mechanic Arts', 'Duties of Masters to Their Apprentices' and 'Electricity'. Among the association's by-laws was a fixed rule against one member employing the apprentice of another if he had run away or broken his arrangement with his master. Finally, to encourage devotion to the trade, the association offered a ten dollar gold medal to any apprentice serving his full term without resorting to drinking strong liquors.[7]

Ever challenged to produce weapons faster and cheaper by the federal government, Armory employees continually improved plant efficiencies, particularly in the area of quality through the usage of precision gages and fixtures. In addition, uniform and rigorous production standards were developed for the many small subcontractors in the region that supplied parts to the Armory, while Armory engineers eagerly provided access to the state-of-the-art manufacturing techniques employed there. Given this opportunity, local firm owners eagerly studied Armory designs, and methods of organization, and thus greatly improved their own plant efficiencies. The Armory's collaborative approach to problem-solving and skill base sank deep roots in the Connecticut River Valley and remained a hallmark of the region well into the 20th century.[8]

Civil War-induced demand led to an expansion of the skilled workforce in the city; Armory output alone jumped an incredible 400 per cent in the first year of the Civil War. At the outset of the war over 3,000 workers were engaged in gun-making, an increase from the approximately 250 before hostilities. By one account rail cars brought hundreds of metalworkers and would-be metalworkmen into Springfield each day from surrounding communities; at war's end many workers became permanent residents.[9] The war also strengthened production relationships between the Armory and other firms in the city and region. An 1861 letter from Springfield mayor Daniel Harris to Armory Director Ripley demonstrates the collaboration that occurred among firms. The James T. Ames Company, one of the biggest suppliers of large cannon to the government during the war, also made production machinery for the Armory. When Mayor Harris learned that the Ames Company was scheduled to make several large cannon for the Armory, he asked Ripley if he might like to have the carriages required to transport the cannon produced in the city as well. Harris concluded his letter by informing Ripley that the Wason Works was just the place 'to get that work well and expeditiously done'; Ripley concurred, and the gun carriages were built locally.[10]

The 'Industrial Beehive' Grows: 1880–1930

The Armory and other Springfield-area machine-making firms and metalworking establishments acted as a 'transmission agency' for the spread of production-enhancing techniques to users in numerous industries.[11] The *American Machinist* (1917) noted that in the Armory '... many good ideas are gathered from the rank and file and it is to the foreman's best interests to bring out the best that is in his men'. Armory historian Patrick Malone concluded that 'successful foremen at Springfield always followed this practice; most of them had risen from the rank and file in the production shop or had served an apprenticeship under a skilled machinist'. This shop culture placed tremendous value on practical experience and encouraged worker participation in machine design and incremental innovation.[12] Springfield became an important industrial centre after the Civil War by building upon its rich skill base and the ever present sources of manufacturing innovation that first the Armory and then other leading machine shops and metalworking firms provided.

By 1880, Springfield led the region in the manufacture of heavy equipment and machinery, with 437 mills and shops employing 7,000 workers. Between 1885 and 1890, machine production rose a remarkable 158 per cent. By 1880, there were factories printing and publishing books, producing envelopes and fine writing paper, sewing machines, church organs, ice skates, paint and chemicals, steam boilers, and fine watches. In 1910, manufacturers employed 12,361 workers in foundries, machine shops, machine tool builders, and electrical machinery firms. A 1913 directory of Massachusetts manufacturers identified eight firms as making automobiles, including bodies and parts; six firms engaged in the manufacture of electrical machinery; and forty firms building machine tools and machine-shop products.[13]

Numerous metalworking firms supported the needs of this diverse manufacturing base for such items as molds, tools, fixtures, slitting knives, nuts, screws, bolts and machinery attachments. For example, the Taylor and Tapley Manufacturing Company, formed from a consolidation of several smaller firms, owned several valuable patents, molds, dies and patterns for the paper collar and cuff industry.

According to a contemporary account, Taylor and Tapley hired skilled workmen in its five-story brick factory who produced shirt collars and cuffs, as well as machinery attachments and large quantities of material for other collar and cuff manufacturers.[14] The R. F. Hawkin's Iron Works, established in the 1840s, built railroad engine-houses and rail bridges. After the Civil War Hawkin's kept a 'large corps of tried and experienced mechanics' at work in its extensive iron foundry, boiler works and machine shops to manufacture bridges, boilers, bolts and forgings for sale to rail lines and manufacturers all over New England.[15]

When trolley lines extended outward from the city's downtown in the early the 1900s, hundreds of new homes were built on streets that carried the names of well-known period automobiles made in Springfield like Knox and Duryea.[16] Manufacturing was clustered in two centers: East Springfield was home to a massive Westinghouse plant and the Stevens-Dureya Car Company, the first automobile factory in the country; the North End, bordered by the Connecticut River to the West and Chicopee to the North, was dotted with dozens of metalworking firms and many small tool and die shops and foundries that specialized in the production of fixtures, tools, and spare parts for these larger companies. Big or small, companies employed mainly skilled machinists, machine operators, and precision assemblers.[17] Springfield's more diversified industrial base continued to serve as a magnet for skilled workers well into the 20th century.[18] For a time the city's diversity of industry and skill base warded off economic upheaval.[19]

One prominent North End firm that drew upon the skills of the city was the Wason Car Manufacturing Company. Established in 1846, Wason produced railroad coaches for virtually every major rail line in the United States and exported to China, Brazil, Venezuela and Canada. At its height in the 1870s, Wason covered over sixteen acres, employed several hundred skilled workers in metalworking, carpentry and cabinetry who produced hundreds of coaches annually. One long-term contract for over 240 passenger, mail, baggage and express cars to the Central Railroad of New Jersey was worth over $1.5 million. Annual sales of the works exceeded $1.5 million by 1875. Along with Wason, the North End housed several other carriage companies, including the Smith Carriage Company, which sold carriages and wagons across the country and in Europe. In 1892, Smith Carriage manufactured the body for the first gasoline powered automobile built in the United States and in 1895 the first major US automobile corporation, the Duryea Motor Wagon Company, assembled its first cars

Figure 3.1 Wason Manufacturing Company, Springfield, Mass.
(Courtesy of the Connecticut Valley Historical Museum, Springfield, Massachusetts.)

in the North End. The Knox Automobile Company and the Indian Motorcycle Company were also incorporated in the 1890s. Both firms were owned in part by the J. Stevens Arms and Tool Company, which built their production machines and tools.[20]

Skill and Springfield's Economic Success

To summarize, integral to the city and region's 19th century and early 20th century success as an industrial center were two historical continuities; the region's ability to design and build machine tools and related accessories, and the large numbers of skilled machinists in the Connecticut River Valley.[21] From the 1830s, Springfield goods producers enjoyed a technological advantage over competitors in other US cities and regions that lacked access to the sources of innovation and skill available there. According to historians David Hounshell and Nathan Rosenberg, the most important 19th-century transmitters of manufacturing innovations were the makers of machine tools, who worked closely with manufacturers in various industries to help them overcome specific production problems. Hounshell notes that as a particular problem was solved, new knowledge went back into the machine tool firms, which then could be used to solve production problems in other industries. From 1830 on, the Armory widely diffused discoveries about mechanized production, especially the utilization of gauges, fixtures, jigs, and dies to insure uniformity of machined parts. It acted both as a clearing house for technical information and a training ground for mechanics who later worked for private arms makers or for other goods producers.

Without the Armory, Springfield was destined to become a transportation center according to Armory historian Derwent Whittlesey. 'The character of the city's industrialism, and the nature of the commodities produced has, however, been largely determined by the activities of the Armory'. Employing highly skilled labor and producing fine grade steel goods, Springfield developed an economic life which, according to Whittlesey, had 'fewer drawbacks than that of most manufacturing cities... As a consequence, Springfield is neither a sleepy village resting on its past glories, nor is it a coarse factory town, conspicuous for its slums and tired workers'.[22]

Well into the 20th century, Springfield firms were recognized for their machinetool innovations and several new firms incorporated there and began to design and build machine tools. In rapid succession, the Stacy Machine Works invented an upright drill, the Bauch Machine Tool Company produced a new series of threading machines, worm gears, universal joints, and cutting tools, and the Hampden Grinding Wheel Company began the manufacture of its own brand of precision grinding wheels. By 1930, Moore Drop Forging Company, incorporated in 1900, was one of the largest firms in the city, with 1,400 workers producing machine beds mainly for the mid-West's huge auto plants. Storms Drop Forge's 1,000 employees manufactured forgings for export world-wide out of steel, brass, and bronze. The Perkins Gear and Machine Company, with 350 skilled machinists, machined precision gears for global export; the Baldwin-Duckworth Company, made high-grade transmission chains for several machine tool builders.

Van Norman Machine Tool, Chapman Valve, and Package Machinery were three Springfield companies with rapidly expanding international markets. Van Norman designed and manufactured grinding machines, milling machines, and machines capable of grinding ball bearings; Chapman Valve operated three large foundries in the city and produced the castings for hydrants, pipe fittings, sluice gates and valves ranging from one-quarter inch to nine feet in diameter; and Package Machinery designed and built automatic package wrapping equipment.[23] By the early 1930s, the Westinghouse Electric and Manufacturing Company was the city's largest manufacturer, with employment averaging 4,000, up from 500 in 1920.

Figure 3.2 Chapman Valve Manufacturing Company.
(*Courtesy of the Connecticut Valley Historical Museum, Springfield, Massachusetts.*)

Springfield's skill base was internationally recognized. In 1919, England's Rolls Royce, Inc. undertook a thorough investigation of potential sites for a new manufacturing facility and chose Springfield. Reasons given for the choice included access to a constant supply of skilled machinists and easy access to high-quality drop forgings. According to Rolls Royce:

> In 1919, Springfield was chosen for the works of Rolls Royce of America, Inc., only after the most meticulous country-wide survey. In addition to being the city freest from labor troubles in the United States, the artisans of Springfield – from long experience in fine precision work – were found to possess the same pride in workmanship as the craftsmen of England.

By the early 1920s, automobiles costing $20,000 were produced by Rolls Royce's 1,400 workers in their North End factory.[24] Henry Ford had similar high praise for the region's metalworkers. According to Ford, 'The skill of Springfield's engineers and workers is traditional. Less well known is the fact that in its world-wide search for never ending improvements, the Ford Motor Company has found in Springfield dependable sources for a substantial portion of its equipment and parts used in building Ford cars'.[25] William Cooper, the Director of the US Bureau of Foreign and Domestic Commerce, noted in 1930 that in Springfield 'the large number of successful firms, including Van Norman, Chapman Valve, Westinghouse, and Bosch relied on worker skills to design and build new equipment and products'. A rich shop-floor skill base, when combined with innovative and forward-looking employers, provided the region with a competitive advantage.[26]

Springfield's employment growth was twice the state average between 1937 and 1947; firms reported shortages of skilled machinists and commenced new training programs. The armory had 500 employees enrolled in evening courses in 1940 and 1,000 in 1941. American Bosch, Westinghouse, and Van Norman established a collaborative program using a vocational high school. But even with these efforts, according to a plant manager of one program-sponsoring firm: 'Skilled mechanics who understand their machines have this year been at a premium. Specialization over a period of many years has led to a large group of just machine operators. They could pull a lever, but that was about it'.[27]

From 'Industrial Beehive' to the 'City of Homes': The Roots of Decline

Precision metalworking allowed Springfield to grow and prosper from the 1930s through the late 1950s long after Massachusetts textile cities like Holyoke and Lowell ceased to prosper. Holyoke, Worcester, and Lowell reached their employment pinnacles in 1919; by contrast, Springfield employment rose dramatically through World War II. From 1939 to 1947, Springfield's production workforce grew almost 62 per cent, doubling the statewide average. However, *c.* 1940–1950, firms began to pass out of local ownership, and thus control, and plant and equipment investments lagged while new owners built factories overseas and in the South, and shifted work to these new facilities. Almost half of all Springfield manufacturing facilities closed between 1947 and 1987.[28]

John Cumbler uses Trenton, New Jersey's motto – "Trenton Makes – The World Takes" as indicative of the manufacturing prowess of the city in the early 20th century. For Cumbler, Trenton's downward spiral is part of a much larger set of political and economic events, the clash between what he terms Civic Capitalism and National Capitalism. The loci of firm control – the board rooms where investment decisions were made and labor negotiation strategies set – slowly migrated from Trenton. 'The social system put together by the entrepreneurs of the nineteenth century was a dynamic system. It was part of a process of social change; once in place, it continued to change both itself and society. The move from civic capitalism, or entrepreneurial individualism, to bureaucratic corporatism, or national capitalism, began in the late nineteenth century and engulfed not just Trenton, but most of the industrial northeast of the United States in the first half of the twentieth century'; Springfield was no exception as we shall see.[29]

William Hartford found a similar dynamic in Holyoke, a neighboring city of Springfield. Lyman Mills, a major employer in the city, closed in 1927 after a vote by the stockholders – the majority of whom were Boston bankers. Southern competition made it unprofitable to invest further in Holyoke. Hartford quotes Old Colony Trust, the major shareholder, 'The amount to be received per share through liquidation conservatively invested would seem to afford better possibilities of return than an investment in the Lyman Mills'. During the 1930s, several more mills closed in the city. In 1938, Farr Alpaca, the city's largest mill with 4000 workers, was liquidated in spite of union wage concessions and an offer of tax abatements if the mill remained in the city. As with Lyman Mills, critical decisions were not made in Holyoke, but by stockholders with no attachments to the city. By 1940, machines had been sold to southern manufacturers and the mills were shuttered. Hartford makes a very important point about these two closings: '... neither company ceased production because of an inability to make a profit. Rather, faced with the need to modernize existing operations, a majority of stockholders believed that the distribution of assets following liquidation would generate proceeds substantially in excess of the current value of company stock'.[30]

Weaknesses in the Springfield economy were impossible to dismiss. Three 1950s closings are symptomatic of the problems faced by the city and region. In July 1954, the Springfield Thread Works, a 52-year-old family business closed its doors. An aging owner was reluctant to invest in new machinery and simply closed the factory in the face of strengthening national competition. Of its 70 employees, ten had worked at the plant over 40 years. In 1958, the meat and provision firm H. L. Handy. Co. announced plans to leave the area, laying off 500 workers. Founded in Springfield in 1883, the company was now one small part of Swift and Company, a national meat packer. Swift stated the closing was a part of its 'program to close uneconomical units, improve others, consolidate operations where possible into the most modern facilities'. The Fleming Foundry, a three generation family-owned business announced it was ceasing operations in March 1959, leaving 50 workers unemployed. Foundries, the starting point for much of basic American industry, were beginning to feel the effects of the national decline in manufacturing.[31]

In 1956, Future Springfield, Inc., a local business and industry group, prepared an economic blueprint for the city. In it they determined that

Figure 3.3 American Bosch, *c.* 1920. Machinists at work in the plant's large Tool Making Department.

(*Courtesy of the Connecticut Valley Historical Museum, Springfield, Massachusetts.*)

Table 3.1 Permanent layoffs and closings of Springfield-area metalworking firms in the mid-1980s–1990s

Company	*Status*	*No. of Jobs Eliminated*	*Closure Dates*	*Years in City*	*Peak Employment since 1960*
American Bosch	Closed	1,500	2/86	80	1,800
Chapman Valve	Closed	250	6/86	100+	2,700
Columbia Bicycle	Closed	250	6/88	80+	1,000
Kidder Stacy	Closed	90	9/89	100+	325
Northeast Wire	Closed	35	1990	22	125
Oxford Precision	Closed	60	9/86	40	120
Package Machinery	Closed	400	9/88	100+	950
Plainville Casting	Closed	65	4/87	65	75
Portage Casting	Closed	60	8/86	36	100
Rafferty Steel	Closed	50	11/85	40	–

Rexnord Roller Chain	Closed	200	6/89	100+	675
Springfield Foundry	Closed	75	4/86	100+	285
Van Norman	Closed	275	10/83	90	1,200
Van Valkenberg Plating	Closed	40	7/86	100+	135
Wico Prestolite	Closed	250	3/82	80	675
Atlas Copco	Layoffs	565	1980s	70+	1,000
Easco Hand Tool	Layoffs	2,000	1980s	75+	2,200
Storms Drop Forge	Layoffs	125	1980s	60+	250

Note: With the exception of Plainville Casting, Rafferty Brown Steel and Oxford Precision, all plants were unionized. Only two of the closed enterprises were locally owned; 15 of the 18 firms had been purchased by outside owners since 1959, and 13 of these had been purchased since 1979.
Source: R. Forrant, 1988. 'Plant Closings and Major Layoffs in greater-Springfield, Massachusetts', Springfield: Machine Action Project.

there were 12 manufacturers that employed over 1,000 people in the city; by 1966, as a consequence of work relocations and closing, the number was eight, and by 1976 there were only five. They would certainly have been distressed to learn that in 1986 just two of their original twelve companies were still in the city.[32] Which plants were likely to close? Table 1 contains a list of the major closing and downsizings in greater-Springfield; several points can be made from the list. All but three of the 15 closed plants were unionized, and just two were still locally owned, though every plant on the list had been under local ownership for at least forty years, six for over one hundred years. Most enterprises had undergone an ownership change within a few years of closing, and in every case the closed plants were the oldest production facilities owned by their new corporate parent. Springfield's now aging industrial enterprises were no match for modern, single-story, better capitalized facilities. The cumulative affect of the closings ended the Connecticut River Valley's reign as a world leader in precision metalworking.[33]

In the 1980s, the shutdown of three long-established metalworking companies – Wico Prestolite, Van Norman, and Chapman Valve – made the deindustrialization crisis inescapable for even the most disinterested observer of the local economy, while the February 1986 announcement that the American Bosch was to close hammered home once and for all the message that the 'industrial beehive' was no more. Wico, founded in Brooklyn in 1897 by Thomas Witherbee, the inventor of the portable storage battery, moved to Springfield in 1904. It was bought and sold three times between 1956 and 1967 before becoming part of the Prestolite division of the Toledo, Ohio-based Eltra Corporation. In the mid-1970s, 530 workers produced electrical and electronic components for small engine ignition systems. Layoffs starting in 1980 cut the workforce in half, and in late 1981 management announced the plant was closing, with all remaining work to be shifted to 'support a marginally profitable operation in the Sunbelt that is located in a modern building with more modern equipment'.[34]

Charles E. and Fred. D. Van Norman, brothers from Hamilton, Ontario, founded the Waltham Watch Tool Company in Watertown, Massachusetts, in 1888. Two years later they moved their business to Springfield and incorporated as the Van Norman Machine Tool Company. Van Norman initially employed 25 workers, producing bench lathes, molding dies, engravers' equipment and other small hand tools. In 1910, the firm's engineers designed and built the first milling machines with adjustable cutter heads and the first cutter grinders. There were ready buyers for these machines in Springfield and in the growing automobile industry. The World War I helped Van Norman gain a national reputation for designing and building a machine that produced ball bearings. Through 1915, ball bearings were largely imported from Germany. US war production would have been crippled without this engineering feat. The company grew through World War II and production focused on machine tools for the automotive industry and multi-purpose milling machines for the global market.[35]

The plant's success caught the attention of New York industrialist Herbert Segal in the early 1950s. Segal wanted to acquire Van Norman for the nucleus of what he hoped would become the 'General Motors of the machine tool industry'. Through the purchase of 35 per cent of Van Norman shares, Segal was able to acquire sufficient power to force several directors off the company board, including surviving co-founder Fred Van Norman. Corporate headquarters shifted to New York City, and Segal began acquiring several smaller machine tool companies. However, the recession of the late 1950s and continued lackluster sales in the early 1960s led to a merger with the Universal American Corporation in 1962 and a second merger in 1967 into the Gulf and Western Corporation. Over this period employment in the Springfield plant fell to 300, from 1,100 in 1958. Finally in 1979, Gulf and Western sold Van Norman to Winona Tool Manufacturing of Winona, Minnesota, and for a time, Winona did some work in Springfield. However, it had acquired the company primarily to utilize Van

Norman's reputation as a premier machine tool builder, the plant shut down in 1983, and Winona began attaching the Van Norman nameplate to imported Italian machines.[36]

Chapman Valve, founded in the 1870s, quickly became one of the leading producers of custom-made valves for large construction projects in the world. By World War II, the company was one of only two US firms building precision valves for submarines. It employed 3,600 in its foundry, pattern, mold making, and machine shops. When Chapman's chief executive died suddenly in 1958, a power struggle ensued, and after two years of behind the scenes machinations Chapman became part of the world-wide conglomerate Crane Corporation. Crane owned a non-union valve plant in Chattanooga, Tennessee, and almost immediately shifted work out of the unionized Chapman to it. At the time of the acquisition Chapman had 2,700 employees, but layoffs, including the closing of the foundry, resulted in there being just 200 workers in the facility mainly doing repair work on valves when it closed in 1986. The Springfield plant had earned the corporation's ire in 1982 when it became the conglomerate's only union plant not to negotiate wage and benefit givebacks.[37]

The Bosch Closing: A Case Study in Demise

The closing of the Bosch plant in 1986 marked the watershed for large-firm metalworking in greater-Springfield. The German-based Robert Bosch Magneto Company constructed one of its first US plants in Springfield in 1911 to take advantage of the city's skilled labor and to gain access to the nation's nascent automobile industry.[38] The plant was seized by the US government during World War I for security reasons and was sold at auction in 1914 to a group of Springfield buyers. Robert Bosch repurchased the plant after World War I and renamed it the American Bosch Company (AB). The workforce grew between the wars and in the mid-1920s the plant employed 2,000 people who produced 50 percent of all the electrical starter parts required by the burgeoning US automobile and truck industries. In the late 1930s, the plant's product mix expanded to include commercial radios, and fuel injection equipment for the aviation industry. Most manufacturers in Springfield, including the Bosch, were non-union until the mid-1930s when the United Electrical, Radio and Machine Workers (UE) successfully organized the firm and several others. Skilled machinists played the lead role in these organizing efforts, and with skills shortages in Springfield machinists gained significant control on the factory floor. This is similar to what Nelson Lichtenstein found in Detroit's automobile plants, but unlike Detroit there was very little disruption of production in Springfield and no evidence of large-scale work stoppages in Bosch during the 1930s and 1940s.[39]

The plant benefited from the surge in war-based production during the 1940s; however, Robert Bosch never gained financially because the US government assumed control of the plant in 1941 through its Alien Property Custodian's Office (APC). After the seizure the Federal Defense Plant Corporation provided $4 million in leased machine tools to the plant to increase production.[40] The magnetos AB manufactured powered virtually every military aircraft built during World War II and its fuel injection equipment could be found in most of the engines powering navy battleships and submarines. Sales climbed to $50 million in 1943 from $13 million in 1941 and employment leapt upward to 6,700 from slightly under 1,000. By 1944, sales reached $61.2 million and employment totaled 7,300. Throughout the war, the APC paid out small stock dividends and set aside $5 million in cash to assist in what it believed would be a costly downward adjustment in the plant to eventual peacetime production.

Bosch emerged from the war as part of the electrical machinery and vehicle components sector of the nation's burgeoning manufacturing economy. At the time it was reasonable for Bosch workers to assume that both the high concentration of UE locals in Springfield and labor's steadfast support for the war effort – there had been no work stoppages during the war – would provide them with a strong bargaining position and job security. However, in Western Massachusetts and Connecticut, 823 military contracts worth approximately $250 million were abruptly canceled and 20,000 workers lost their jobs in the early Fall of 1945. Erratic employment swings tied to defense spending became a constant in the region for the next several years.[41]

The APC sold the plant in 1948 for $6 million to AMRA, a two-year old financial holding company headed by Charles Allen, the president of the Wall Street investment firm Allen and Company. The holding company's board of directors included the major partners of several Wall Street legal firms as well as the presidents of the American Securities Corporation and the American Overseas Development Corporation.[42] In 1949 Allen merged the Bosch with ARMA Corporation, a Long Island, New York defense electronics firm, to form American Bosch-ARMA (ABA), with headquarters on Long Island. Bosch was now just one of several production facilities owned by a financial holding concern whose growth strategy was predicated upon product and market diversification, cost cutting at its existing facilities, and the construction of low-wage, non-union plants in the South. The switch from localized ownership, with at least some concern for the well-being of the Springfield plant and workforce, to ownership with the ability to play off against one another the interests of several production facilities in a search for maximum profits, commenced the downward slide to closure in 1986.[43]

All high volume automotive work was relocated to a new plant in Mississippi in the early 1950s. In a letter to workers that announced the change management for the first time raised the issue of national wage competition. The company president noted that a move of some work to a low-cost area was essential if the company was to maintain a competitive advantage in the manufacture of its products. The letter stated that, ‘When one or more companies start producing in an area where operating costs are much lower, other competitive companies in the same field also have to move in order to survive. It is either move or quit’.[44] In 1959 workers were warned of global wage pressures in a letter that read in part ‘American Bosch's foreign competitors enjoy a greater and too frequently a decisive cost advantage over us... A major cost factor is of course labour costs’. Workers were informed that, ‘For every dollar earned by an AB employee an employee of a foreign competitor is paid an average of only 25 cents. This means that where our average hourly rate is $2.66 the comparable hourly rate in West Germany is 66 cents, in Japan 27 cents and only 80 cents in the United Kingdom’.[45]

In the early 1960s management considered purchasing all components from German, Japanese and English suppliers, with only diesel assembly work to remain in Springfield. However, work remained in

Figure 3.4 Newspaper, cartoon from April 1954.

Springfield because corporate officers were unable to locate a skilled labor pool at lower wages, while defense-related orders increased and needed to be completed in the US. Though Springfield's defense work was on the upswing warning signs persisted as commercial business slumped. Determined to control labor costs and diversify away from diesel and defense, the corporation launched an aggressive acquisition campaign and purchased: Bacharach Instruments and Packard Instruments, US leaders in the production of electronic measuring and testing instruments for medical and radiation research; Pace Industries, a Tennessee defense manufacturer; Michigan Dynamics, a producer of scientific and medical instruments; and European leaders in the production of a full range of factory automation equipment, Hispano Suiza in the Netherlands and Steelweld in Great Britain, between 1966 and 1969. A joint production agreement reached with the British conglomerate DeHaviland Holdings Ltd, established a presence in important European defense and automotive markets.

The European acquisitions were part of a dramatic increase in domestic disinvestment and capital reallocation by US corporations. Total overseas direct investments in factories, office buildings, machine tools, and office equipment, less than $50 billion in 1965, reached $124 billion in 1975, and surpassed $213 billion by 1980. According to economists Barry Bluestone and Bennet Harrison profits from these investments jumped from $5.2 billion in 1965 to more that $424 billion in 1980. Plant closings in the US became endemic, and by Harrison and Bluestone's calculation 'over the whole decade of the 1970s, a minimum of 32 million jobs were probably eliminated in the United States as a direct result of private disinvestment in plant and equipment'. Beck's investments were part of ABA's corporate strategy to reduce production costs at the expense of the Springfield workforce and gain access to European markets and were similar to the strategic business choices made by hundreds of other US corporations at the time.[46]

The threat of permanent job loss was a potent weapon in the corporation's arsenal and the wild swings in employment in the 1950s and 1960s attested to the fact that the company could and would lay-off large numbers of workers (see Figure 3.5). This fear of job loss surely prodded many workers to participate in management's cost improvement program, established in 1956. Under the program workers were encouraged to submit ideas to 'lower costs, improve working conditions or in some way improve the quality of American Bosch products'. However, management inexplicably ordered that the union's two committee representatives could attend just four monthly meetings a year. In spite of the dissension, this caused worker suggestions saved the company over $1.5 million in the first year.

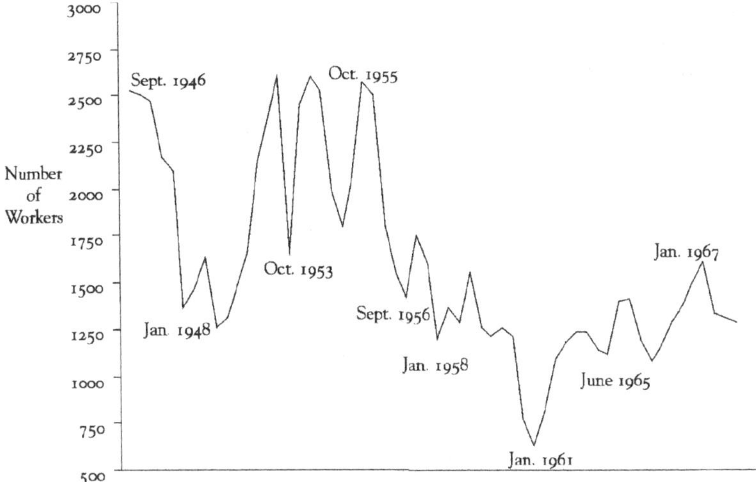

Figure 3.5 Local 206 Membership 1946–1968.

Between 1957 and 1960 over $10 million was invested in new machine tools, many with state-of-the art numerical controls capable of performing several machining functions with only limited operator intervention. Management was convinced that the machines would make it easier for engineers to measure the time required to produce finished parts, and thus help production managers to gain grater control over work flow and to increase productivity. The acquisitions were utilized throughout the early 1960s to displace skilled workers, and the union's initial happiness with the investment turned sour, much the same as it did with the improvement program. 'Battery of new operator-eliminator machines being set up rear of Department 160', read a union newsletter. 'There will be so much new machinery by July of next year that there will undoubtedly be fewer people working here. Automation means – Meet the market competition by fewer Union members'. Management's improvement program and automation efforts were castigated as a ploy to get workers to participate in their own speed-up and were dubbed the 'consolidate effort – eliminate personnel' campaigns by unionists.[47]

The defense boom waned in the late 1960s with resultant sharp employment cuts, and at the same time the corporation constructed factories in Italy and Holland to manufacture several newly designed diesel fuel injection systems for the automotive and agricultural equipment market. This decision was a serious blow to Springfield's future, since the prototype development and experimental machining for these products was completed locally. Thereafter, a noticeable shift in market orientation away from diesel and defense work through the stepped up acquisition of several companies in the scientific and medical instrumentation fields, took place. As a result of this changed corporate focus and the drop in defense spending, diesel and aerospace sales fell to $45 million from $73 million between 1968 and 1971. Over the same period scientific and medical instruments sales jumped to $36.6 million from $22.6 million, and electronics rose to $26 million from $20 million (for net sales by division, see Table 2). In 1970, the corporation was renamed AMBAC Industries as the Bosch name disappeared from the title and the 1971 Annual report celebrated the fact that '27 percent of total sales and 40 percent of total profits came from scientific, medical, environmental, and industrial instruments, products all acquired or developed in the last five years'.[48]

The need for Bosch workers' expertise became less relevant when much of the remainder of the fuel injection work was shifted to the Netherlands and Italy in the mid-1970s. Management once again pressed the issue of labor costs, arguing that wages needed to be dramatically lowered if the plant was to be competitive in the global economy, while machines were taken off the shop floor and shipped with what had once been Springfield's work to corporate factories and joint ventures now scattered around the world. The company's 'reduced costs' argument carried no weight with the rank-and-file and was viewed as a 'make the workers pay' approach to resolving problems in the plant. Several bitter strikes in the 1970s surely hastened management's decision to exit the plant once and for all.[49]

Finally, in the early 1980s the plant's last owner, the aerospace giant United Technologies, built a state-of-the-art plant in Columbia, South

Table 3.2 Corporate net sales in millions by division 1964–1971

	1964	*1965*	*1966*	*1967*	*1968*	*1969*	*1970*	*1971*
Diesel Systems	27.7	33.9	40.6	43.6	48.1	47.9	34.0	30.0
Electrical Products	13.4	14.9	17.4	16.4	19.9	21.6	21.7	26.0
Scien./Med. Inst.	11.6	13.7	18.1	22.5	22.6	26.4	32.3	36.6
Aerospace	31.2	25.4	32.0	28.5	25.6	20.7	20.5	14.8
Industrial Products	3.6	3.8	4.7	8.2	12.3	12.2	16.9	10.6
Ordnance					22.5	31.2	30.4	16.8

Carolina, to perform the remainder of the work in Springfield. The end came swiftly and in the words of 36-year plant veteran Donald Staples 'It's not like they pulled the rug out from under us, it's more like they pulled the trap-door out from under the hangman's noose'.[50] On February 4, 1986, set aside as the first day to commence a round of contract negotiations, United Technologies corporate officers handed union representatives a terse twenty-line memo that stated in part:

> We are unable to continue operating four facilities with this continuing over-capacity situation. I therefore, regret to inform you that a very difficult business decision has been made to close the Springfield manufacturing operation by the end of August of this year. The military products will be moved to Columbia, South Carolina; injectors to Brescia, Italy; and industrial products to Fluid Power of the Components Division.[51]

Between February and August, 1,200 people were terminated and machinery was moved to other United Technologies locations. Today, in the North End there is only one manufacturer still in operation. Block after block of triple-decker wood-frame apartment buildings, first home to the thousands of workers who made their way to Springfield have burned down, been torn down, or are in total disrepair. In a neighborhood that had teemed with working class pubs and diners are a refuse recycling center and a low-rise office building housing lawyers, a cable television company, a medical complex, and eight industrial smokestacks, stark reminders of the physical boundaries of a once thriving industrial center.

Summary and Conclusion: The Rebirth of Skill and Collaboration

In the 19th century Springfield became a diversified manufacturing region dotted with small and medium-sized metalworking companies which collectively employed thousands of engineers and skilled and semi-skilled machinists, producing machine tools, assemblies, and components for the nation's machine tool, automobile, steel, and electrical equipment industries. These firms were supported by small, highly specialized tool and die shops and foundries engaged in the production of fixtures, tooling, gauges, and made-to-order components. By the 1870s, a second industrial concentration had grown up around the Wason Car Manufacturing Company. The machine making and metalworking industries were "transmission agencies" that spread innovation in a particular application to users in entirely different industries.

Nineteenth and early twentieth century metalworking growth stemmed from three related factors: continual innovation in product design and development stimulated initially by the Springfield Armory; a diverse nucleus of locally owned, collaborative, machine tool builders and precision metalworking firms whose expertise provided the region with immediate benefits from their technological breakthroughs, and a base of skilled workers (many of them German, Scottish, and British immigrants) capable of performing the precision machining required to turn out world-class products. The region's strength was embodied in the rich problem-solving capabilities shared by firms and their workers.

Declining economic performance after World War II should have become a widely discussed public issue, especially with the release in 1951 of a study of the New England economy by President Harry Truman's Council of Economic Advisers. In Springfield, industrial production contracted significantly after 1945. According to one local account: 'In 1929, 47,700 people worked in city factories. In 1941, the number reached more than 54,000 and Springfield was designated one of thirty-two war production centers'.[52] However, between August and late December 1945, Springfield Armory employment dropped sharply: on V-E Day there were 9,900 civilian employees there, by V-J Day 4,440, and by end of 1945 only 1,700 workers remained.[53] The council expressed its concern that New England firm owners had turned away from industrial progress.

> To some extent manufacturing success in the 19th century and the early part of the 20th century seems to have bred lethargy and complacency among New England industrialists, which handicapped the region it its competition with newer regions. The gap between ownership policies motivated by short-run financial considerations and the need for long-run modernization, research and product development has also intensified manufacturing problems in New England.[54]

The impact of this changed behavior was felt in Springfield. Merrit Roe Smith argues that in the early and mid-19th century geographic proximity and accessibility to new machine tools and knowledge sharing gave Springfield and other Connecticut River towns production advantages. However, by the early 1950s, skill development, technological innovation, and the diffusion of new production methods lessened throughout the city and region. There was little evidence of the types of collaboration found earlier, either between firms, or between managers and workers. Management determined that there was little to gain from maintaining relationships with shop-floor workers which included worker participation in production-related decision-making.

The skill base was once the foundation for a vibrant economy, but with that skill base under attack production advantages were lost.[55]

The purchase of firms by conglomerates exacerbated the erosion of shop-floor skills, as one after another, firms made the ruinous decision to disband apprenticeship programs, cut back on worker training, and concentrate instead on training foremen to 'get the work out'. Skill, and by implication, historical knowledge of the production process, was marginalized; machine tools, it was reasoned, could serve as able stand-ins for highly skilled machinists and metalworkers. The president's council had determined that regional solutions for the slowing New England economy depended on recapturing the earlier production advantages derived from technological innovation and employee skills; however, this was not what took place in greater-Springfield. The city contained many aging, multi-story factories that were no match for the new, one-story facilities being constructed across the South. The 'fools-gold' of defense spending during the Korean War rearmament boom and the Viet Nam War allowed firms and workers to ignore their internal and external problems, but this was hardly enough to stimulate sustainable growth or fend off the plant closings to come in the 1970s and 1980s. Already in the 1960s city officials had renamed the 'Industrial Beehive the 'City of Homes'.

Thirty-five years after the Council of Economic Advisers report and in the face of persistent blue-collar job loss in greater-Springfield, the Machine Action Project was established by the Commonwealth of Massachusetts' Executive Office of Labour and strategies began to be employed to 'remake' the industrial base. Ironically, the original intent of the project was to transition the region out of metalworking toward service industries. However, staff research quickly revealed that an extensive network of small metalworking firms had maintained a presence in the region despite the large-firm closings, and that several cities and towns still had 30 percent or more of their private sector employment in metalworking.[56] Over the next six years, MAP acted as a catalyst between the region's small metalworking firms, local education and training providers, and state and federal agencies, to provide industry-focused training and technical assistance to hundreds of managers and workers employed in the region's metalworking industry.

MAP identified a nucleus of firm owners concerned about the future of the industry and these owners became part of MAP's advisory board. For the owners, participation on the board was their first experience interacting with economic development practitioners and public officials on a sustained basis. The local chapter of the National Tooling and Machining Association (NTMA) was to play a lead role in this group.[57] Staff visited 100 firms over a six-month span to determine the strengths and weaknesses of companies and to assess whether owners and community actors were willing to work together to revitalize the metalworking industry. A database of some 350 firms (employing 15,000 workers) was established. The visits made it clear that firms often interacted in quite coherent ways to accomplish specific production-related tasks. Firms subcontracted extensively to one another regardless of size; five-person shops were sending work to fifty-person shops and vice versa.[58]

Rather than transition displaced workers out of the industry altogether, MAP staff and its industry-led Board of Directors determined that the program should nurture the small firm base. The numerous plant-closings suggested an overabundance of machinists in the region, yet a paradox emerged from the visits because firm owners lamented that they were unable to fill job openings. A comparative survey of the skills of several hundred laid-off workers and those individuals employed in small shops explained this discrepancy. Workers losing their jobs in the region's large firms were machine operators who lacked the setup, blueprint-reading, and math skills required by the small precision shops. Firms produced small-lot sizes, which meant frequent setups, and workers who needed to operate several different types of machine tools; such flexibility had not been required in large firms like the Bosch which produced long runs of the same product. Research had determined that small firms provided a link to the original strength of the regional economy, the skill base.

A comprehensive program consisting of the following interrelated components has been in place since 1988: interfirm learning activities including management seminars, networking projects and monthly presentations on management strategy, new product development, and quality issues; Evening Skills Upgrading Courses for workers and managers running the gamut from basic math and blueprint reading to advanced CNC programming and just-in-time management techniques; MechTech, a four-year apprenticeship program, combining academic and work-based learning resulting in an associate's degree in manufacturing technology and a journeyman's certificate; a 23-week training course in intermediate/advanced machining to prepare unemployed individuals for entry-level employment in precision machine shops; and in-plant assessments and technical assistance projects to modernize shop operations.[59]

The slow, steady regeneration of the greater Springfield metalworking region today rests upon a continuous and disciplined social process characterized by research, discussion, shared learning, reflection, and experimentation among firms, their trade association – The National Tooling and Machining Association – and several public agencies. The strength of the firms acting collectively on their own behalf was dramatically enhanced when strict attention was paid to the realities of the region's industrial history, and the region's long-term reliance on a rich skill base was recognized. While after the Word War II the Springfield metalworking region was never dominated by *Fortune* 500 corporations, it was dominated by firms with 1,000–2,000 employees for nearly a 50-year period. From the end of Word War II through the late 1980s, the region lacked the technological-diffusion capacity of the earlier period, and one after another, firms ended their apprenticeship programs, therefore the skill base dissipated. Skill, and by implication, historical knowledge of the manufacturing process, became expendable; machine tools, it was reasoned, could serve as substitutes for highly trained workers. If skills were needed, it was cheaper in the near-term to simply offer more money to a worker from a neighboring firm, than invest in an in-house or collaborative regional apprenticeship program. The decline of the larger enterprises challenged the remaining small firms to rebuild, and an understanding of the industrial history of the region helped to set in motion a new dynamic, based on skill development, technology diffusion and interfirm learning reminiscent of the days when the region truly was an 'industrial beehive'.

Notes

1 C. Antonelli and R. Marchionatti, 'Technological and organisational change in a process of industrial rejuvenation: The case of the Italian cotton textile industry', *Cambridge Journal of Economics*, 22 (1998), pp. 1–18; W. Hartford, *Where Is Our Responsibility? Unions and Economic Change in the New England Textile Industry* (Amherst: University of Massachusetts Press, 1996); A. Wieandt, 'Innovation and the creation, development and destruction of markets in the world machine tool industry', *Small Business Economics*, 6 (1994), pp. 421–37; V. Capecchi, 'In search of flexibility: The Bologna metalworking industry, 1900–1992', in C. Sabel and J. Zeitlin (eds), *World of Possibilities: Flexibility and Mass Production in Western Industrialization* (New York: Cambridge University Press, 1997), pp. 381–418; J. Saglio, 'Local industry and actors' strategies: From combs to plastics in Oyonnax', in C. Sabel and J. Zeitlin (eds), *World of Possibilities*, pp. 419–60; D. Angel, *Restructuring for Innovation: The Remaking of the US Semiconductor Industry* (New York: The Guilford Press, 1994); P. Scranton, *Endless Novelty: Specialty Production and American Industrialization, 1865–1925* (Princeton, NJ: Princeton University Press, 1997); J. Brown, *The Baldwin Locomotive Works 1831–1915: A Study in American Industrial Practice* (Baltimore: The Johns Hopkins University Press, 1995). For empirical studies of present-day regional industrial clusters and how firms and regions develop competencies, see the special issue of *Regional Studies*, 'Regional Networking, Collective Learning and Innovation in High Technology SMEs in Europe, 33 (1999); A. Herod, 'From a geography of labor to a labor geography: Labor's spatial fix and the geography of capitalism', *Antipode*, 29 (1997), pp. 1–31; P. Scranton,

'Webs of productive association in American industrialization: patterns of institution-formation and their limits, Philadelphia, 1880–1930', *Journal of Industrial History*, 1 (1998), pp. 9–34.

2 M. Frisch, *Town into City: Springfield, Massachusetts and the Meaning of Community: 1840–1860* (Cambridge: Harvard University Press, 1972). Springfield's industrial growth was jeopardized briefly, when at the conclusion of the Revolutionary War Congress decided to relocate the armory ten miles across the Connecticut River at West Springfield, where a facility was to be built to harness the power of the Agawam River. However, after protests against this move by large numbers of West Springfield farmers the Armory remained in Springfield, and that city, rather than West Springfield, benefited from the economic stimulus the Armory soon provided. The Armory was described by one British visitor as 'beautifully situated on an eminence overlooking the town', see N. Rosenberg (ed.), *The American System of Manufactures: The Report of the Committee on the Machinery of the United States 1855 and the Special Reports of George Wallis and Joseph Whitworth* (Edinburgh: Edinburgh University Press, 1969), p. 364. For an historical analysis of pre-Civil War industrialization in New England that compares the role of merchants in the Lowell textile paradigm with the role of merchants in Springfield, see François Weil, 'Capitalism and industrialization in New England, 1815–1845', *The Journal of American History* (1998), pp. 1334–54.

3 D. Hounshell, *From the American System to Mass Production, 1800–1932* (Baltimore: Johns Hopkins University Press, 1984), pp. 33–4, 44. Hounshell points out that two keys to Armory success were an early reliance on private arms contractors as a source for innovation and the perfecting of various ways to inspect parts in the process of manufacture. This concept spread to other metalworking establishments in Springfield and over time added to the region's reputation for high-quality work. Hounshell also cites F. Deyrup's *Arms Makers of the Connecticut Valley* (Northampton, MA: Smith College Studies in History Series, 1948) for its documentation of instances when the Armory's patternmakers and skilled foundrymen made machine casting for many area machine tool builders without the internal capacity to do so.

4 F. Deyrup, *Arms Makers*, p. 66.

5 Frisch, *Town into City*, p. 15. The city grew 400 percent between 1820 and 1850, third highest in the state. Further North along the Connecticut River there was a thriving cutlery and hand tool industry, boosted by sales to the military for bayonets and burgeoning markets for agricultural implements. Cutlery firms took advantage of advances in the area in grinding wheel technology. By one account an obstacle to growth was a persistent lack of all-around skilled workers equipped with the diversity of knowledge required by firms. An apprenticeship program was started, in addition firms recruited workers from Sheffield, England. There was also an upsurge of immigration to the region from Germany in the late 1840s and early 1850s, M. Van Hosen Taber, *A History of the Cutlery Industry in the Connecticut Valley* (Northampton, MA: Smith College Studies in History, 1955).

6 See J. W. Roe, *English and American Tool Builders* (New York: McGraw Hill Book Company, 1926). Roe has several genealogies of industries that trace the movement of key personnel from plant to plant in the 19th century. For the interconnections in the Connecticut River Valley, p. 139 and for Worcester, Massachusetts, p. 223.

7 M. Green, *Springfield Memories: Odds and Ends of Anecdote and Early Doings* (Springfield: Whitney and Adams, 1876), pp. 54–5. The ten dollar gold piece offer proved so successful that it was abandoned when in one year 32 apprentices were eligible and the association's treasury was not large enough to make the promised pay-out.

8 Frisch, *Town into City*, p. 74; D. Whittlesey, *The Springfield Armory: A Study in Institutional Development* (unpublished Ph.D. Dis., University of Chicago, 1920), p. 265; D. Meyer, 'Formation of advanced technology districts: New England textile machinery and firearms', *Economic Geography*, Extra Issue (1998), pp. 31–45. Meyer notes that the early fire arms industry in greater-Springfield capitalized on 'the technical skills already in the region, embedded in small forges, foundries, and mechanical workshops that provided diverse metal goods for the prosperous economy' (p. 42). Palfrey, *Statistics of the Condition and Products of Certain Branches of Industry in Massachusetts for the Year Ending April 1, 1845 (1846)*. For a look at the Armory and how its production methods and shop floor organization influenced manufacturing, see M. Best, *The New Competition* (Cambridge: Harvard University Press, 1990).

9 M. King, *King's Handbook of Springfield, Massachusetts: A Series of Monographs Historical and Descriptive* (Springfield: James D. Gill, 1884), pp. 35–7.

10 Frisch, *Town into City*, p. 79.

11 N. Rosenberg, 'Technological change in the machine tool industry, 1840–1910', *Journal of Economic History*, 23 (1963), pp. 414–46. The development and diffusion of skills through movements of skilled workers within and across industries represents one example of how learning systems developed during the 19th century. Much research needs to be done to trace the career patterns of skilled machinists and the pioneers in machinery design.

12 P. Malone, 'Little kinks and devices at the Springfield Armory, 1892–1918', *Journal of the Society for Industrial Archeology*, 14 (1988), pp. 55–71. Malone notes that the Armory's sop culture placed a great value on practical experience, promoted shop-floor participation in machine design and incremental innovation and 'encouraged respect for the ideas of 'practical men' p. 64.

13 Commonwealth of Massachusetts, *A Directory of Massachusetts Manufacturers* (Boston, MA, 1913). The automobile builders included Knox Automobile, Atlas Motor Car, Sultan Motor Company and Springfield Metal Body Company and the Wason Manufacturing Company. To date very little has been written about what happened to these firms. The firms engaged in the manufacture of electrical machinery included the Bosch Magneto Company. Machine tool firms included Bausch Machine Tool, Chapman Valve, and Van Norman Machine Tool. By 1930, greater Springfield manufacturers accounted for 75 percent ($308 million) of the total value of all manufactured products produced in the Connecticut River Valley, see K. Lumpkin, *Shutdowns in the Connecticut River Valley* (Northampton: Smith College Studies in History Series, 19, April, 1934), pp. 150–1.

14 King, *King's Handbook*, pp. 333–4.

15 King, *King's Handbook*, pp. 336–7.

16 For photographs of early Springfield factories, see D. J. D'Amato, *Springfield – 350 Years: A Pictorial History* (Virginia: The Donning Company, 1985).

17 D'Amato, *Springfield – 350 Years*, p. 139.

18 The Bosch company newsletter aptly titled *The Craftsman* contains evidence of the role highly skilled workers played in production. The December 1948 issue carried the names of forty-nine workers who had reached twenty-five years seniority in the factory. Seventeen of the forty-nine were foreign born, including six from Germany and four from Italy. Among the group were four toolmakers, three die makers, two set up men, a production engineer, and the foreman of the experimental machine shop (*Craftsman*, 5, no. 8). Issues of the *Craftsman* from 1944–1958 are located in the Pioneer Valley Historical Society company archives, Springfield, Massachusetts.

19 On the eve of World War II greater-Springfield had close to 200 specialty machine shops and metalworking firms producing precision components and machine tools. Figures taken from the *Fifteenth United States Census* show that the three largest sectors were the iron and steel industry with 4,900 workers; the electrical machinery industry with 2,710 workers; and miscellaneous manufacturing with 4,400. According to a 1941 Work Projects Administration Study of Springfield: 'Springfield's products have been for the most part the essentials of other industries, the machines, the tools, and units that turn the wheels of industry the world over. Because of this inter-relationship and the diversification of her industries, Springfield has suffered less from economic upheaval than single-industry cities of New England'.

20 For a discussion of eighteen prominent late 19th century Springfield manufacturers, see King, *King's Handbook*, pp. 319–70.

21 Planning Services Group, *The Regional Economy; Federal Population Census, 1920, 1930, 1940.*

22 Rosenberg, 'technological change'; Hounshell, *From the American System*, pp. 33 –4, 44. Hounshell cites Felica Deyrup's *Arms Makers of the Connecticut Valley* (Smith College Studies in History, 1948) for its documentation of instances when the Armory's patternmakers and skilled foundrymen made 'castings of valuable machines developed by contractors' p. 45; Whittlesey, *The Springfield Armory*, p. 265.

23 O. Stone, *History of Massachusetts Industries: Their Inception, Growth, and Success* (Boston: S. J. Clarke Publishing Company, 1930), p. 539. Package Machinery formed in 1912 as the result of a merger of several smaller companies based in Springfield, Milwaukee, Wisconsin, Louisville, Kentucky, Chicago, Illinois and New York City and Brooklyn, New York. The merger was designed to eliminate costs associated with each firm's pursuing parallel technology and to establish greater production efficiencies.

First year sales were $140,000; by 1930 they approached $2 million.

24 Stone, *History*, p. 550.

25 *SR*, November 21, 1936, p. 13.

26 Cooper, forward to Charles Artman, *The Industrial Structure of New England* (Washington, DC, 1930), xi. The report is based on information gathered from close to 5,000 manufacturers regarding methods of manufacturing, plant organization and marketing strategies supplemented by Federal manufacturing census data. It contains richly detailed analyses of the metalworking, machine tool building, textiles, leather, paper, printing and publishing and wood and furniture industries.

27 *Springfield Republican*, October 25, 1936.

28 R. Forrant, *Metalworking Plant Closings and Major Layoffs in Hampden County, 1967–1986* (Springfield: Machine Action Project, 1987); US Department of Commerce, *Manufacturing Censuses.* For the Holyoke story on mill ownership changes and disinvestment, see W. Hartford, *Working People of Holyoke* (New Brunswick: Rutgers University Press, 1990), see esp. ch. 8.

29 J. Cumbler, *A Social History of Economic Decline: Business, Politics and Work in Trenton* (New Brunswick: Rutgers University Press, 1989), p. 5.

30 Hartford, *Working People of Holyoke*, pp. 191–3.

31 *SMU*, July 24, 1954, p. 10; *SDN*, August 21, 1958, p. 1; *SMU*, March 5, 1959, p. 13. See R. Forrant, 'The cutting edge dulled: the post-Second World War decline of the United States machine tool industry', *International Contributions to Labour Studies*, 7 (1997), pp. 37–58, for a discussion of the rapid demise of the machine tool industry in the 1960s and 1970s. Forrant cites several factors contributing to the decline including: a failure of firms to invest sufficiently in new products and manufacturing processes; an inability to manage erratic business cycles; a failure to capitalize on important new technology developments like computer controls for machinery; an inability to establish and maintain effective collaborations among the host of quite small firms that made up the bulk of the industry; and a failure to invest in workforce development as evidenced by the abandonment of apprenticeship programs at scores of the nation's premier tool builders.

32 Future Springfield, Inc. *Report* (1956) found in Pioneer Valley Historical Society Business Collection series. The 12 are American Bosch, Chapman Valve, Gilbert and Barker, Package Machinery, F. W. Sickles, Springfield Armory, J. Stevens Arms, US Rubber, Van Norman Machine, Westinghouse, Monsanto Chemical, and Spaulding. Only the last two are still in operation. R. Forrant, *Metalworking Plant Closings.*

33 R. Forrant, E. Cann and K. McGraw, *Industrial District or Industrial Decline? A Survey of Western Massachusetts Metalworking* (Springfield, 1991). There are currently less than 15 unionized metalworking firms in the region, each much smaller than it was in the 1950s. Each has engaged in concession bargaining and made numerous changes in such things as their incentive system, and seniority and classification language, areas that produced the greatest conflicts in the Bosch. There are now various efforts underway to work with the remaining small firms to help them find markets to replace the loss of defense work. There are also several programs to improve training to preserve the dwindling skill base. It should be noted that the average age of a skilled machinist in Western Massachusetts is 55.

34 Forrant, *Metalworking Plant Closings.*

35 Forrant, *Metalworking Plant Closings.*

36 Forrant, *Metalworking Plant Closings.* Van Norman's demise is similar to that of another US machine tool builder, Burgmaster, richly described in M. Holland, *When the Machine Stopped: A Cautionary Tale from Industrial America* (Cambridge, Harvard Business School Press, 1989). Holland writes that in the 1960s, because of their profits and seeming hold over the market, US tool builders became enticing targets for conglomerates. He estimates that two-thirds of the industry was affected. The end result of this process was that 'A distant managerial capitalism replaced entrepreneurial capitalism...', p. 266.

37 Forrant, *Metalworking Plant Closings.* By the late 1970s, Crane was getting large valves cast in overseas foundries at a fraction of the Springfield cost, using patterns designed and built in the Springfield pattern shop by highly skilled machinists and designers.

38 Founded in 1886 in Stuttgart by Robert Bosch, the company achieved rapid growth between 1900 and 1915 with Bosch's invention of a high-voltage magneto to create an electrical supply for the internal combustion engine. In 1915, the company employed over 5,000 workers and was the largest manufacturer in South Germany. Early photographs of the Springfield facility show hundreds of lab-coated machinists utilizing their skills in the production of electrical parts for the emerging automobile and truck industries.

39 Photographs taken as late as the mid-1930s show skilled machinists in shirt and tie at their work benches in the Bosch tool and die shop. In 1936, tool room workers were the nucleus of the United Electrical Worker's successful union organizing effort. The UE used this base in Springfield to launch successful unionization efforts up and down the Connecticut River Valley from Bridgeport, Connecticut to Springfield, Vermont. This group of workers, many Scottish and Germany immigrants, also ran an unsuccessful campaign for mayor and several city council seats in Springfield in 1935 with the establishment of the Springfield United Labor Party. The party's mayoral candidate was Westinghouse tool and die maker, Matthew Campbell. The party sought to shift the tax burden from small-home owners to large industries and pledged to give preference to locally produced products in all city purchases. By 1939, UE represented workers across the Northeast who were responsible for the output of 80 percent of US electrical goods, from the smallest appliances like toasters and fans to the largest electrical generators built in the world. R. Forrant, 'Skilled Workers and Union Organization in Springfield, Massachusetts: The American Bosch Story', *Historical Journal of Massachusetts*, 24 (1996), pp. 47–67; *UE News*, 7 January 1939, pp. 4 –5. On the role of skilled workers in union formation see P. Leahey, 'Skilled labor and the rise of the modern corporation: the case of the electrical industry', *Labor History*, 27, no. 1 (1985–86), pp. 31–53; S. Meyer, 'Technology and the workplace: skilled and production workers at Allis-Chalmers, 1900–1941', *Technology and Culture*, 29 (1988), pp. 839–64; N. Lichtenstein, *The Most Dangerous Man in Detroit: Walter Reuther and the Fate of American Labor* (New York: Basic Books, 1995).

40 *Springfield Morning Union* (SMU), 14 February 1941; 27 March, 22 June 1942. The APC's Leo Crowley had control over the stock and could sell it at his discretion. In 1942, at the insistence of the Treasury Department, 23 employees were terminated as security risks, including the vice-president for product development and 12 engineers.

41 During the immediate post-war years Springfield labor was also rocked by the bitter internal strife that broke out in the American labor movement over the alleged role of Communist Party members and sympathizers in several national unions, tore apart trade union unity in Springfield. The split was swift, as in just eight weeks during November and December 1949 every UE local in the city disaffiliated with it to join the fledgling and unabashedly anti-communist International Union of Electrical Workers (IUE). For this history, see R. Forrant, *Skill Was Never Enough: American*

Bosch, Union Local 206, and the Decline of Metalworking in Springfield, Massachusetts 1900–1970 (unpublished Ph.D. dissertation, University of Massachusetts, 1994).

42 The sale was a particularly lucrative one for the holding company since at the time of purchase the plant was valued at $13.5 million and the cash reserves that the APC established during the war reached $5 million.

43 In 1953, construction of a new plant commenced in Mississippi. In a letter to workers that for the first time raised the issue of wage competition, the company president stated that a move of some work to a low-cost area was essential if the company was to maintain a competitive advantage in the manufacture of high volume automotive components like windshield wiper motors. The letter noted that, 'When one or more companies start producing in an area where operating costs are much lower, other competitive companies in the same field also have to move in order to survive. Its either move or quit' (Donald Hess letter quoted in Forrant, *Skill Was Never Enough*, p. 72).

44 Forrant, *Skill Was Never Enough*, p. 72.

45 Forrant, *Skill Was Never Enough*, p. 119.

46 W. Lazonick, *Competitive Advantage on the Shop Floor* (Cambridge: Harvard University Press, 1992), pp. 283–4; B. Bluestone and B. Harrison, *The Deindustrialization of America: Plant Closings, Community Abandonments and the Dismantling of Basic Industry* (New York: Basic Books, 1988), pp. 26, 35; Forrant, *Skill Was Never Enough*, p. 244.

47 Forrant, *Skill Was Never Enough*. Burgmaster multispindle drill presses capable of performing up to eight separate drilling operations without removing a part from its fixture were located in six departments. The company newsletter noted that with these machines no worker attention is needed 'except to load, press the start button, and unload. This permits the operator to operate a second machine'. Kingsbury horizontal drilling machines were acquired and, according to management, 'Working back-to-back, two units are capable of drilling, counter-sinking, and tapping up to 26 holes simultaneously'.

48 AMBAC, *Annual Report*, 1971; AMBAC, *Securities and Exchange Commission Prospectus*, 1971.

49 For an examination of union – management conflict in the Bosch, R. Forrant, '"Quality and Selling Price Go Hand in Hand, Like Ham and Eggs, Toast and Butter": American Bosch, Local 206, and the Blunting of Shop-floor Participation 1950–1970', *International Contributions to Labour Studies*, 6 (1996), pp. 1–27.

50 *Springfield Morning Union*, February 5, 1986, p. 1.

51 *Plant Closing Memorandum*, February 4, 1986, American Bosch Local 206 files, University of Massachusetts Amherst.

52 D'Amato, *Springfield – 350 Years*, p. 141.

53 Green has a lengthy description of these training efforts. Green, 413–416; Springfield Armory Historical Summary of Activities 2 September 1945–30 June 1951, p. 103.

54 Council of Economic Advisors, 1951, xxii. M. Best and R. Forrant, 'Community-Based Careers and Economic Virtue', in M. Arthur and D. Rousseau (eds), *The Boundaryless Career: A New Employment Principle for a New Organization Era* (New York: Oxford University Press, 1998), pp. 314–30.

55 See R. Forrant, 'Quality and selling price go hand in hand'; M. R. Smith, *Harpers Ferry Armory and the New Technology: The Challenge of Change* (Ithaca: Cornell University Press, 1977), pp. 104–5.

56 For an extended discussion of MAP, see R. Forrant and E. Flynn, 'Seizing agglomeration's potential: the Greater Springfield Massachusetts metalworking district in transition, 1986–1996', *Regional Studies*, 32 (1998), pp. 209–22. In spite of the documented closings, there still remains a metalworking corridor in western Massachusetts that stretches north into Vermont and south through Connecticut. By counts of firms and workers, it is still one of the largest concentration of such firms in the United States; for cluster maps see B. Harrison, M. Kelley and J. Gant, 'Innovative firm behavior and local milieu: Exploring the intersection of agglomeration, firm effects, and technological change', *Economic Geography*, 72 (1996), pp. 233–58. For a map that depicts the intensity of machine tool building in the United States in 1915, see Roe, *English and American Tool Builders*, p. 279. One of the largest concentrations of firms was in the Connecticut River Valley.

57 The National Tooling and Machining Association (NTMA), located in Washington, DC, is the national representatives of approximately 3,000 custom precision manufacturing companies throughout the United States. There are 55 local chapters of the NTMA located throughout the country. Member firms pay fees directly to the national chapter and local chapters receive a 20 percent return on these dues. Local chapters operate 13 regional training centers for toolmakers and machinists. Since 1970, the western Massachusetts chapter of the NTMA has operated the Western Massachusetts Precision Institute.

58 Forrant and Flynn, 'seizing agglomeration's potential', pp. 212–3. The Machine Action Project governing board was comprised of five firm owners, five union officers, three local economic development officials, two representative of the banking community, the president of the local two-year technical college, instructors from local technical high schools and members of the business press.

59 Forrant and Flynn, 'seizing agglomeration's potential'. In the theoretical literature on regional development, there is an emerging consensus that while the agglomeration of firms carries with it the potential, it does not automatically lead to an acceleration of education, training, and learning in and across firms. Firm density alone does not promote positive performance, and in the Springfield case in the mid-20th century the density acted as a catalyst to widespread decline. For a sampling of the literature see, A. Amin and K. Robins, 'The reemergence of regional economies? the mythical geography of flexible accumulation', *Environment and Planning D*, 8 (1990), pp. 7–34; R. Florida, 'Regional creative destruction: production organization, globalization, and the economic transformation of the midwest', *Economic Geography*, 72 (1996), pp. 315–35; A. Markusen, 'Studying regions by studying firms', *Professional Geography*, 46 (1994), pp. 477–90; C. Sabel, 'Bootstrapping reform: rebuilding firms, the welfare state, and unions', *Politics & Society*, 23 (1995), 5–48; A. J. Scott, 'The geographic foundations of industrial performance', *Competition and Change*, 1 (1995), pp. 51–66.

Retrospective

Robert Forrant

For over 150 years, the 200-mile industrial corridor along the Connecticut River between Bridgeport, Connecticut, and Windsor, Vermont, produced an innovative economy, resulting in skilled workers gaining a high degree of wage stability and intergenerational advance. For example, from the mid-19th century through approximately 1975, Greenfield, MA, was a world center for precision toolmaking at the heart of the region. The shop-floor skill base and innovative and forward-looking employers produced a competitive advantage: the region was a skill magnet!

The sharp decline of manufacturing in the United States, which accelerated after 1970, directly impacted machinery builders and firms engaged in the manufacture of precision metal parts. The glory days of manufacturing were the 1970s. Nearly 20 million Americans earned their pay from factory work; in 2020, roughly 12 million workers do so. Outside investors and conglomerates who had purchased the region's leading firms in the 1950s and 1960s felt no obligation to the Valley's workers and managers as decline set in. The Valley's industrial disassembly set in motion a downward spiral decimating every manufacturing city's economy.

However, after a period of next to no growth, the region's manufacturing is witnessing a rebirth. Output and employment are up. University of Massachusetts Donahue Institute researchers note that many precision parts Massachusetts manufacturers make are hidden inside other products, i.e., shafts for machines that create flu vaccines, medical testing equipment, lens housings for night-vision goggles, sensors for submarines and robots. In 2015, Deloitte Consulting LLP described what it referred to as New England's manufacturing revolution. Critical components of this renaissance include workforce development and the emergence of a 'tightly integrated ecosystem of partners in industry, government and education'.

Such a conjunction is highly reminiscent of the characteristics that shaped the Connecticut River Valley's success nearly 150 years ago. While jobs will never reach the levels maintained from the 1940s through the early 1970s, the nascent revival offers an opportunity for workers once more to receive wages and benefits commensurate with their knowledge. Ironically, regional economy analysts agree that a powerful brake on further expansion is the lack of highly skilled machinists.

Index

Note: **Bold** page numbers refer to tables; *italic* page numbers refer to figures and page numbers followed by "n" denote endnotes.

9780367023911